D0867163

Cherokee Prehistory

Cherokee Prehistory

THE PISGAH PHASE IN
THE APPALACHIAN SUMMIT REGION

By Roy S. Dickens, Jr.

THE UNIVERSITY OF TENNESSEE PRESS

KNOXVILLE

GARDNER-WEBB COLLEGE LIBRARY
P. O. Box 836
Boiling Springs, N.C. 28017

E
99
.C5
D52

Copyright © 1976 by The University of Tennessee Press / Knoxville.
All rights reserved. Manufactured in the United States of America.
Second printing, 1981

Library of Congress Cataloging in Publication Data

Dickens, Roy S. Jr. 1938-
  Cherokee prehistory.

  Bibliography: p.
  Includes index.
    1. Cherokee Indians—Antiquities. 2. Indians
of North America—Appalachian Mountains, Southern
—Antiquities. 3. Appalachian Mountains, Southern
—Antiquities. I. Title.
E99.C5D52   970'.004'97   76-1972
ISBN 0-87049-193-8

To the Memory of
Bill and Elizabeth Klein

Preface

After a century of archaeological research in the southeastern United States, there are still areas for which we do not have even preliminary coverage. Surprisingly, one of these areas is the interior region of the Southern Appalachian Mountains—the Appalachian Summit —which in historic times was inhabited by the Cherokee people whose rich culture and wide influence made their name commonplace in typifying Southeastern Indians. The culture of the people who preceded the historic Cherokees was no less rich, and their network of relationships with other groups no less wide. But, until recently, the prehistoric cultural remains of the Southern Appalachians had not been systematically explored.

Archaeological sites in the mountains do not stand out dramatically on the landscape as do the effigy mounds of the Ohio Valley and the massive platform mounds of the Southeastern Piedmont and Mississippi Valley, and perhaps to the eye of the early researcher there seemed to be nothing important to dig. Prehistoric settlements in the Southern Appalachians lay in the bottomlands along the clear, rocky rivers, hidden in the folds of the mountains. Finding and investigating the sites of those settlements required a systematic approach. From 1964 to 1971, under the direction of Joffre L. Coe, the Research Laboratories of Anthropology at the University of North Carolina, Chapel Hill, conducted a Cherokee Archaeological Project, funded by a grant from the National Science Foundation. The project was designed to investigate the antecedents of the historic Cherokees in the Appalachian Summit, and included site surveys over large portions of the region and concentrated excavations at several important sites in the area of the historic Cherokee Middle and Out towns.

One result of the Cherokee Project is this book, the purpose of which is to present an initial description and synthesis of a late prehistoric phase in the Appalachian Summit, a phase that lasted from the beginnings of South Appalachian Mississippian culture to the emergence of identifiable Cherokee culture. At various points through the study I shall try to draw these data into the broader picture of Southeastern prehistory, and I shall even venture some interpretations of the human behavior behind the material remains. But the reader must keep in mind that my primary purpose is to make available some new information on a previously unexplored area. At the least, this type of presentation of the archaeological record can provide a necessary first step to approaching, in specific ways, the problems of cultural process and systemics in the aboriginal Southeast.

I am indebted to a number of people for contributions to this study. Foremost among these is Joffre L. Coe, who directed the Cherokee Archaeological Project and was chairman of my doctoral committee. Dr. Coe provided continual instruction, advice, and friendship, and he allowed me to include data from several aspects of the project in which I was not directly involved. The late William G. Klein, Professor Emeritus of Sociology and Anthropology at Warren Wilson College, deserves special recognition. Dr. Klein brought the Warren Wilson site to our attention and worked closely with us during three field seasons. His interest, enthusiasm, and untiring energy were instrumental in turning a six-week text excavation into an ongoing archaeological field school.

I also wish to express my gratitude to President Arthur Bannerman, Dean Henry Jensen, Elizabeth Klein, Ernst Larsen, Samuel Miller, Roger Stuck, Mark Trumbo, and the numerous others at Warren Wilson College who worked on behalf of "the dig." The field crews at the Warren Wilson site were composed of students from Warren Wilson College and the University of North Carolina. The names of these students, together with the years that each one participated in the project, are as follows:

Mitchell Arney	1967	Theresa Godfrey	1966, 1967, and 1968
Jennifer Baird	1967	Sterling Hopper	1967
Stanley Bates	1968	Steven Jones	1966
Robert Bowers	1967 and 1968	Robert Keeler	1968
Jane Braun	1966	Earl LeQuire	1966
George Brookshire	1966	Cynthia Love	1967
Catherine Brutsch	1967	Dale Morris	1968
William Collins	1967	Ruth Neal	1968
Ila Mae Cox	1966	Janice Reinhard	1966
Douglas Dellinger	1966	Patricia Sanford	1968
Raymond Dunton	1966 and 1967	Ulys Smith	1966 and 1967
Wilma Eliassen	1967 and 1968	Judy Summey	1968
Elizabeth Evans	1968	Kathleen Surber	1967

| Christa Thomas | 1968 | James Willis | 1967 and 1968 |
| Ann Tony | 1967 | Jane Willis | 1966 and 1967 |

I received able assistance in the field and laboratory from Veletta Canouts, Robert Keeler, John Mattson, Patricia Sanford, Ulys Smith, and Frank Weir. To my colleagues who worked on other aspects of the Cherokee Project—Brian Egloff, Keith Egloff, Leland Ferguson, John Halsey, Bennie Keel, Olin McCormick, Vance Packard, and J. Jefferson Reid—I am indebted for constant intellectual stimulation and occasional "spiritual" uplift.

My appreciation goes to Richard A. Yarnell for his analysis and report on the plant remains from the Warren Wilson site (Appendix 1), and to Elizabeth Wing for her analysis and report on the faunal remains (Appendix 2); they both also commented on Chapter 6. I am also grateful to Jon Muller for his commentary on the shell gorgets.

Information on various sites and collections was graciously provided by Wesley Breedlove, Jr., Joseph R. Caldwell, John T. Dorwin, Charles H. Faulkner, Leland G. Ferguson, Roger T. Grange, C. G. Holland, James H. Kellar, A. R. Kelly, Lewis H. Larson, Jr., James H. Polhemus, Richard R. Polhemus, and David C. Smith.

Credit is due Jefferson Reid for Figure 12; Frank Weir for Figure 15; and Olin McCormick and Joan Rupp for assistance on the photographic plates. Donald Brockington, Joffre Coe, Leland Ferguson, and Jane Packard read a first draft of the manuscript and made critical comments. Carol Dickens deserves a special thanks for undertaking the typing and proofreading of several drafts of the manuscript. Thurla McCash assisted in the typing of the final draft.

Contents

Illustrations

PLATES

PLATES

FIGURES

TABLES

Cherokee Prehistory

1. Introduction

Despite widespread interest in Cherokee Indian culture by historians, anthropologists, and others, much of the interior region of the Southern Appalachians—the heartland of the historic Cherokees—has remained virtually unknown archaeologically. This deficiency, however, has not kept scholars from speculating about the origins and evolution of Cherokee culture. Such speculations have been variously based on ethnohistorical documents, linguistics, Indian legends, and a limited amount of archaeological data.

My objective here is to present a body of information on a newly discovered late prehistoric archaeological phase in the Appalachian Summit region. This phase has been assigned the name Pisgah. Discussions will center on several categories of Pisgah remains—sites, structures, features, burials, artifacts, ceramics, and food remains. Much of the data comes from two major excavations in western North Carolina—the Warren Wilson and Garden Creek sites[1]—but other excavations and surface surveys provide additional information.

Comparative and distributional analyses of the artifacts and other remains are undertaken to determine generalized temporal and spatial boundaries for the Pisgah phase and to indicate relationships to other contemporary Southeastern cultures. Specific traits, such as those manifest in the ceramics, are examined in terms of their possible development within the local sequence and with regard to their possible derivation through interaction between Pisgah and neighboring cultures.

An important aspect of the study naturally relates to the problem of the origins of Cherokee culture. In this regard, traits of the Pisgah phase are compared with traits known to be associated with the historic Cherokees, the intention being to detect patterns of

1. I was field supervisor at the Warren Wilson site during the summers of 1966, 1967, and 1968. Data from the 1969 excavations at this site were provided by Veletta Canouts. Information on excavations at the Garden Creek site was provided by Bennie Keel, Leland Ferguson, and Jefferson Reid. Joffre Coe was in overall supervision of both excavations.

continuity or change from the late prehistoric to the historic periods. I undertake such an enterprise with the recognition that attempts to link archaeological cultures with ethnographically described cultures are hazardous at best.

Terms for cultural classification will be used, essentially, as they are by Willey and Phillips (1958). Briefly, a *component* defines a body of related archaeological remains found usually within a single layer on a site; a *culture* denotes a recurring component, i.e., a body of related remains repeated on more than one site within a given area; a *phase* delimits the temporal duration of a culture; a *pattern* refers to the spatial extent of a group of related cultures; and a *tradition* stands for a temporal continuity of related cultures. All of these terms carry the implication of social and ideological relationships beyond the material remains.

THE APPALACHIAN SUMMIT REGION

The Blue Ridge Province of the Appalachian Highlands extends from southern Pennsylvania to northern Georgia. That portion from southwestern Virginia to northeastern Georgia—which includes the broadest and most rugged extent of mountainous terrain—has been termed by physiographers the Southern Blue Ridge (Thornbury 1965) and by anthropologists the Appalachian Summit (Kroeber 1939). It includes all of far-western North Carolina, along with portions of extreme eastern Tennessee, southwestern Virginia, northeastern Georgia, and northwestern South Carolina (Figure 1). The emphasis in this study is on western North Carolina, this being the portion for which the greatest quantity of archaeological information is presently available.

The Appalachian Summit, a sprawling confusion of mountain ranges, stands in marked contrast to the low hills that border it on the east and south and the consistent ridges and broad valleys that border it on the west. The eastern margin is formed by the Blue Ridge escarpment, which has the highest elevations in the eastern United States and serves as the drainage divide between the Atlantic Ocean and the Gulf of Mexico. To the west of this escarpment, the Great Smokies, Unakas, and other ranges, together with intervening coves, basins, and narrow river valleys, form a complex topography.

The Appalachian Summit is drained largely by tributaries of the Tennessee River, among the more important of which are the Hol-

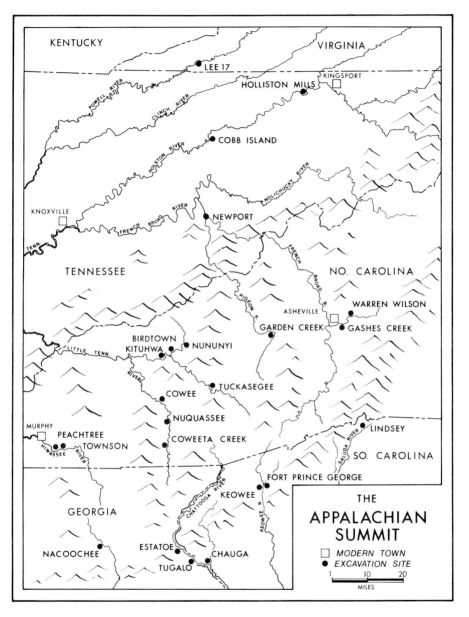

FIGURE 1. The Appalachian Summit and some important sites.

ston, Nolichucky, French Broad, Pigeon, Little Tennessee, and Hiwassee. Headwaters of the Saluda, Keowee, Chattooga, and Chattahoochee rivers impinge on the southern margins. These upland streams usually do not have the wide valley courses and extensive alluvial plains such as those associated with streams in the adjacent Ridge and Valley and Piedmont provinces. This type of topography does not support dense agricultural populations in modern times, and was probably a factor in the distribution of aboriginal populations.

The Appalachian Summit is characterized by a patchwork of contiguous microenvironments, each having marked variation in climate, soils, flora, and fauna.[2] For example, a mountain slope and its adjacent valley floor can differ as much as three weeks in growing season and several degrees in mean annual temperature. Rainfall is highly variable, with yearly averages ranging from as little as 40 inches in some areas to as much as 80 inches in others. Soils are equally divergent, with young, alluvial and erosional soils occurring on low slopes, terraces, and valley floors, and mature soils being found at higher elevations.

In aboriginal times, much of the area was forested. Oak-chestnut and oak-pine forests occupied intermediate slopes, rolling hill country, and intermontane basins; mixed mesophytic communities were found on low slopes and in moist coves; and northern hardwoods and spruce-fir stands occupied higher elevations. A broad range of shrubs and herbs was found within these forests. Animal life was equally varied. Mammals of economic importance ranged from small species, such as squirrel, rabbit, raccoon, opossum, beaver, fox, bobcat, wolf, and mountain lion, to the larger deer, black bear, and occasional elk and bison. Turkey and various other birds were found year-round, and there were migrant ducks and geese in winter. Numerous species of insects, fish, shellfish, amphibians, and reptiles were also present.

HISTORY OF APPALACHIAN SUMMIT ARCHAEOLOGY

The record of archaeological research in the Appalachian Summit is one of sporadic and scattered work, some of which was never

2. The following characterization of the Appalachian Summit environment was taken from Braun (1964), Shelford (1963), and Peattie (1943).

compiled into formal reports. The earliest documented excavations were those conducted for the Smithsonian's Bureau of Ethnology in the 1880s. Most of these projects were restricted to the Tennessee River Valley, west of the Summit, where sites richer in mounds and burials were to be found. The results of this work were reported by Cyrus Thomas (1887, 1890, 1891, 1894) and W. H. Holmes (1884, 1903), both of whom concluded that the archaeological remains were products of ancestral American Indians. These archaeologists helped lay to rest the theory of an extinct race of "Mound Builders" advanced by earlier writers, and they even went so far as to propose a strong connection between the prehistoric cultures and the later Cherokees.

At the same time as the Smithsonian projects, investigations of sites in western North Carolina were conducted by the Valentine Museum of Richmond, Virginia. Mann S. Valentine directed his sons, aided by local residents, to excavate mounds in Haywood, Jackson, Swain, and Cherokee counties. One of their smaller excavations was at Garden Creek Mound No. 2, in Haywood County, a site of recent importance. When the Valentines compared the pottery found in this and other mounds with the ceramics still being made on the Qualla Reservation, the striking similarities led them to conclude (1898:53) that the mounds were built by a "civilization" akin to that of the historic Cherokees.

Unfortunately, when the Valentines' work was only shortly under way, they became involved in an elaborate deception that misdirected their interpretations of the archaeological remains. Local opportunists made and sold to them, and to Smithsonian representatives, a number of stone carvings that were claimed to have been unearthed at ancient mountaintop sites. Completely taken in by this hoax, Mann Valentine speculated that the carvings were the work of a prehistoric "race" distinct from the Mound Builders. None of the Valentine research was ever published, but an extensive log of field notes, correspondence, and interpretive manuscripts, and the bulk of their archaeological collections, are preserved.[3]

In 1915-1919, the Museum of the American Indian-Heye Foundation conducted excavations at the Garden Creek site (Heye 1919), at the Nacoochee Mound in northern Georgia (Heye, Hodge, and Pepper 1918), and at several sites on the upper Tennessee River

---

3. Photocopies of the documents and most of the artifacts from western North Carolina sites are on file at the Research Laboratories of Anthropology, University of North Carolina, Chapel Hill.

(Harrington 1922). There seems to have been a consensus among the Heye Foundation archaeologists that the ancestors of the Cherokees had long inhabited the Southern Appalachians (Heye, Hodge, and Pepper 1918:13, 56; Harrington 1922:281-298).

In 1933-1934, extensive excavations were carried out by the Smithsonian Institution at the Peachtree site on the Hiwassee River in Cherokee County, North Carolina. By the time this work was published, culture period designations of "Woodland," "Mississippian," and "Historic" were in use in the Southeast, and the authors observed that even though all three periods were represented at Peachtree, there was little evidence for long-term abandonments or major cultural discontinuities. They concluded that the various remains were part of a common tradition, and that the latest of these remains represented "the material culture of a group of Cherokee inhabiting the site" (Setzler and Jennings 1941:12).

Following the Peachtree excavations, there was little archaeological activity in the Appalachian Summit. Work on the periphery of the region produced some valuable information, but when researchers tackled the "Cherokee problem" there was a divergence of interpretations. Several writers (Webb 1938; Lewis and Kneberg 1946; Caldwell 1955) even suggested that the Cherokees were recent migrants into the southern mountains. In 1961, Joffre Coe (59-60) summed up the confusion with the following statement:

> For the most part, the conclusions regarding the [origins of the] Cherokee have come about as the byproduct of work oriented toward other problems . . . . I do not believe, however, that work on the periphery will ever solve the heart of this problem. A thorough investigation of the Middle and Valley towns of the Cherokee must be completed before many of the present questions can be answered.

Coe began an intensive program of survey and excavation in western North Carolina in 1964. Preliminary to large-scale investigations, site surveys were initiated in several of the mountain counties as early as 1958. Through these surveys, many new sites were discovered and an effort was made to locate historically documented Cherokee towns. Collections obtained at this time were used to set up tentative artifact typologies and to compile valuable distributional data.

In 1964, limited excavations were conducted at two historic villages—the Tuckasegee site in Jackson County and the Townson site in Cherokee County (Coe and Keel 1965; Keel 1972), and in 1965, more extensive work was commenced at two mound-and-village sites—the Garden Creek site in Haywood County and the Coweeta Creek site in Macon County. Excavations at the former site were concluded in 1967, whereas work at the latter was continued until 1971. In 1966, excavations were begun at a prehistoric village site located on the campus of Warren Wilson College in Buncombe County. At the time of this writing, work at the Warren Wilson site is being continued each summer.

During the period of the Cherokee Project, in addition to the above work, test excavations, surface surveys, and visits to private collections were carried out, and these provided valuable distributional and chronological data. Also, there were correlative studies of pertinent historical documents (e.g., Dickens 1967a).

OUTLINE OF THE WESTERN NORTH CAROLINA ARCHAEOLOGICAL SEQUENCE

As a result of the Cherokee Project and other recent investigations, a general picture of the archaeological sequence in the Appalachian Summit is emerging. Although the spatial and temporal extent of every cultural unit is not yet completely defined (and there are even some large gaps in the data), it is possible nevertheless to present an outline of the sequence as it is presently understood (Table 1).

PALEO-INDIAN PERIOD (ca. 10,000 B.C.-8000 B.C.)

Fluted, lanceolate projectile points, usually identified with the Paleo-Indian period in other parts of eastern North America, have been found in several of the mountain counties (Perkinson 1971). Although most of these artifacts have been observed in private collections, they occur with enough regularity to indicate that there was human activity over most of the Appalachian Summit prior to the Archaic period.

ARCHAIC PERIOD (ca. 8000 B.C.-1000 B.C.)

Chipped stone artifacts similar to ones found in Early and Middle Archaic assemblages on the Carolina Piedmont have been reported at a number of western North Carolina sites. Projectile point types

Table 1. Archaeological Sequence in the Appalachian Summit Region.

DATE	PERIOD	PHASE
1838	Removal	
		Late Qualla
1650	EURO-AMERICAN	
		Early Qualla
1450		Late Pisgah
1000	MISSISSIPPIAN	Early Pisgah
500	Middle	Connestee
A.D.0 B.C.		Pigeon
500	Early	Swannanoa
1000	WOODLAND	
2000	Late	Savannah River
5000	Middle	Morrow Mountain
8000	Early	?
	ARCHAIC	
?	PALEO-INDIAN	?

include Hardaway, Palmer, Kirk, Le Croy, Stanly, Morrow Mountain, and Guilford (Coe 1964). Such points were found by Keel (1972:65) in excavations at the Tuckasegee site and by Holden (1966:50-54) in surface contexts at a number of sites in Transylvania County. At the Warren Wilson site, Morrow Mountain points were found in the oldest cultural deposits.

Late Archaic remains have a broad distribution in the mountain area. Holden (1966:50-54) found Savannah River points on several sites in Transylvania County, and the same type of point occurred in excavated contexts at the Tuckasegee site (Keel 1972:34-83), the Gashes Creek site (Dickens 1970:15), and the Warren Wilson site. At Warren Wilson, the Savannah River component overlay the Morrow Mountain component and contained large stemmed projectile points, grooved axes, pear-shaped manos, mortars, hammerstones, and fragments of soapstone vessels. These artifacts were associated with basin-shaped pits filled with small river boulders and charcoal.

WOODLAND PERIOD (ca. 1000 B.C.-A.D. 1000)

The Woodland period in the Appalachian Summit is marked by the beginnings of pottery making and the introduction of the bow and arrow. These, along with other changes in technology, subsistence, and social organization, were elaborations on a pattern well developed in the preceding Late Archaic period.

A clearly defined Early Woodland component on a number of sites has been termed by Keel (1972) the Swannanoa phase. Holden (1966:60-64) was the first to describe Swannanoa pottery, which she called the "Early series" and classified as Early Cord Marked and Early Fabric Marked. Keel has also recognized simple stamped, check stamped, and smoothed plain finishes, which he believes were late additions to this phase as a consequence of increased cultural interaction with the Southern Piedmont region (Keel 1972: 298-299). The artifact inventory of the Swannanoa phase also includes small stemmed projectile points, bone awls, expanded-center bar gorgets, soapstone vessels, pitted and pebble hammerstones, net weights, tubular ceramic pipes, and pigment stones. At the Warren Wilson and Gashes Creek sites, these artifacts were found in association with clusters of fire-fractured rocks in deposits that overlay the Late Archaic deposits. This phase has been estimated to date 700 B.C.-200 B.C. (Keel 1972:310).

Two Middle Woodland phases have been defined for the Appalachian Summit. The earliest of these is designated the Pigeon phase (Holden 1966; Keel 1972). Keel (1972:295-298) proposes that the development of Pigeon ceramics was part of a northward spread of Deptford-type paddle stamping. Vessels are check stamped or simple stamped, and have crushed quartz temper and tetrapodal supports. Other artifacts include small, side notched projectile points, flake scrapers, bone and antler awls, hammerstones, celts, expanded-center gorgets, and stone and ceramic pipes. Stone-lined pit hearths are recorded, but there is little information at present on dwelling structures, burials, or subsistence practices. Remains of the Pigeon phase were found in contexts overlying those of the Swannanoa phase at Garden Creek Mound No. 2 and at the Warren Wilson site. A dating of ca. 200 B.C.-A.D. 300 has been suggested (Keel 1972:308) for the Pigeon phase.

The terminal portion of the Middle Woodland period is represented by the Connestee phase (Holden 1966; Keel 1972). This phase is distinguished by sand tempered pottery with finishes that are usually plain, brushed, or simple stamped, but occasionally may be cord marked, fabric marked, check stamped, or complicated stamped. The complicated stamped motifs strongly resemble Napier Complicated Stamped of the Georgia Piedmont (Wauchope 1966: 57-63). Also present are small side notched and triangular projectile points, flake scrapers and gravers, stone discs, conical celts, tabular gorgets, elbow and platform pipes, grooved stone plummets and pendants, small cylindrical hammerstones, bone awls, cut deer mandibles, and abraded pigment stones.

In addition to this "local" assemblage, a group of artifacts of "exotic" materials was found in association with the Connestee occupation at Garden Creek Mound No. 2. Keel describes and interprets these important items:

> A Hopewellian derived assemblage was associated with the Connestee occupation. Evidence for this association was found in the upper third of the pre-mound layer, but more convincingly in the primary and secondary mounds. This assemblage consisted of prismatic blades, polyhedral cores, triangular knives (cache blades), sheet copper, copper beads, a bi-pointed copper pin, human and animal figurines, and certain pottery types. Only the figurines and perhaps some of the Turner Simple Stamped pottery could have been produced from local materials.

> The association of this assemblage with the Connestee phase is a matter of serious concern, since it will necessitate a re-evaluation of Southeastern-Hopewell interaction. The thesis offered is that the apogee of this inter-

action occurred during the Middle and Late Hopewell-Connestee period, not in the preceding Early Hopewell-Mossy Oak-Deptford-Pigeon period [Keel 1972:212].

Garden Creek Mound No. 2, begun in the Connestee phase, served as a platform for a small rectangular building. A number of refuse pits, burned areas, and rock-filled hearths were also associated with this mound (Keel 1972:106-113). One of these pits, presumed to be late in the Connestee occupation, was radiocarbon dated A.D. 805 ± 85 (GX0593).

Information on Connestee settlement and subsistence patterns is limited. However, evidence at Gashes Creek and Garden Creek Mound No. 2 suggests a relatively stable village settlement, and preliminary analyses of charred vegetal remains indicate that a broad range of local plants was collected and that possibly there was some incipient farming (Keel and Chapman n.d.).

The superposition of Connestee phase artifacts over those of the preceding Woodland and Archaic phases was clearly documented by the deposits at Garden Creek Mound No. 2, the Warren Wilson site, and the Gashes Creek site. Keel (1972:289-294) proposes that the Connestee phase is related to the Roan-Rhea complex, Candy Creek complex, and Hamilton focus of eastern Tennessee and to late Hopewellian sites in Ohio, and he supports convincingly an interpretation of Connestee as "a development from earlier local manifestations [in which] the strong southern influence apparent in the preceding Pigeon phase diminished and interaction seems to have been directed to the west and northwest." A suggested dating of this phase is A.D. 300-1000 (Keel 1972:286).

MISSISSIPPIAN PERIOD (ca. A.D. 1000-1650)

Some traits which were to be common in the Mississippian period, such as rectilinear complicated stamped pottery and platform mounds, were already present in the Appalachian Summit in the late Connestee phase of the Middle Woodland period. After about A.D. 1000, these traits, along with a nucleated-village settlement pattern, maize agriculture, and a stratified social structure, brought the Appalachian Summit cultures into a generalized South Appalachian-Mississippian pattern (Ferguson 1971). The first division of the Mississippian period is designated the Pisgah phase (ca. A.D. 1000-1450). It is very probable that the Pisgah archaeological assemblage described in the following chapters, especially those remains from the Warren Wilson and Garden Creek sites, represents a late subphase (ca. A.D. 1250-1450) in the Pisgah development. It seems, therefore, that a major gap in our information exists between the latest of the well-described Middle Woodland phases and the majority of the Pisgah assemblage presented in this study. The probability of this gap is further supported by the fact that, for western North Carolina, the only radiocarbon date for Connestee is A.D. 805 ± 85 (GX0593) and the only date for Pisgah is A.D. 1435 ± 70 (GX0595), a difference of about 630 years.

The early Qualla phase (Egloff 1967) followed the Pisgah phase over most of the Appalachian Summit. In western North Carolina, this phase has been identified in all but the easternmost of the mountain counties, with information coming from numerous surface surveys and from excavations at Garden Creek Mound No. 1 in Haywood County and the Coweeta Creek site in Macon County. It is tentatively dated A.D. 1450-1650.

Early Qualla ceramics are characterized by a combination of older Pisgah attributes along with additions from the more southerly Lamar style. Large bowls and jars with bold complicated stamping, check stamping, and incising are characteristic (Egloff 1967:34). Other artifacts include small triangular projectile points, flake scrapers and drills, rectanguloid celts, stone and potsherd discs, stone and clay elbow pipes, bone awls, and antler flakers.

The typical building was of wattle-and-daub construction, with a roughly square or occasionally circular plan, bark-covered or thatched roof, and central clay fire basin. A ceremonial or civic structure might be a little larger than the domestic structure and possibly erected on an earthen platform. At the Coweeta Creek site (Egloff 1971), a small village was tightly clustered around a civic precinct that consisted of a plaza with a mound and its superstructure at one end and a secondary ceremonial structure at the opposite end.

The economy of the early Qualla phase has not been adequately studied thus far, but the available evidence points to maize-bean-squash cultivation, supplemented by hunting, fishing, and gathering. Flexed burials, in straight-walled and chambered pits, are found in house floors and in the floors of mound structures. Grave accompaniments include marine shell beads, gorgets, ear pins, and dippers, along with fancy clay pipes, polished stone discs and celts, and caches of chipped stone projectile points.

EURO-AMERICAN PERIOD (ca. A.D. 1650 to Removal)

By the late 1600s, there were fixed and regular trade relationships between the Cherokees and the recent migrants from Europe.
This period is characterized by the late Qualla phase, which has
been identified at a number of historically documented Cherokee
towns (Egloff 1967). Important excavated sites include the Tuckasegee site (Coe and Keel 1965; Keel 1972), Garden Creek Mound
No. 1, the Coweeta Creek site (Egloff 1971), and the Townson site
(Coe and Keel 1965).

Late Qualla ceramics are very similar to those of the early Qualla
phase, as is much of the material culture. But in addition to the indigenous elements, we find European-made items such as glass trade
beads, iron tools and utensils, guns, glass bottles, and copper kettles.
A transition during this phase from the aboriginal dwelling structure
to a European-type cabin with horizontal rail walls has been revealed by archaeology (Coe and Keel 1965) and contemporary doc-
umentation (Bartram 1791:296). Ceremonial and civic structures,
however, seem to have remained essentially unchanged until nearly
the end of the historic period (see descriptions of council houses,
Bartram 1791:284, 296-299; Timberlake 1765:59), but less effort
was expended in the maintenance and enlargement of platform
mounds. The overall settlement pattern seems also to have changed,
during the 18th century, from one of nucleated towns to one in
which houses were only loosely grouped, usually in a linear plan. By
the early 19th century, widely scattered, individual homesteads
were the rule (Wilms 1974).

Increasingly, after 1650, the Cherokees depended upon a trade
economy induced by the Europeans, and they became unavoidably
involved in Euro-American politics and wars. Many of the changes
from early to late Qualla can be attributed to this process of accul-
turation. At first the native technology, economy, and settlement
patterns were altered, and ultimately there was an erosion of the
social, political, and religious systems.

2. Sites, Structures, and Features

A Pisgah component has been recorded on more than 300 sites in the Appalachian Summit and adjoining areas.[1] Information on many of these sites comes from surveys and from scattered references in unpublished field records and early published reports. Even though the data are incomplete, the basic attributes of Pisgah settlement organization, domestic and ceremonial architecture, and other habitation features can be reconstructed from the excavations at the Warren Wilson and Garden Creek sites.

A comparison of the characteristics of Pisgah architecture and settlements with those of neighboring, contemporaneous cultures suggests a broad distribution of certain traits in the Southern Appalachians, and confirms that Pisgah played a distinct role in the development of the settlement patterns and ceremonial architecture of the historic Cherokees.

CHARACTERISTICS OF PISGAH SITES

Pisgah sites, according to current survey data, are most numerous in the upper valleys of the Holston, Nolichucky, French Broad, Pigeon, Tuckasegee, Little Tennessee, Catawba, Keowee, and Saluda rivers. Other sites have been found as far north as Lee County, Virginia, as far west as Knox County, Tennessee, as far south as Oconee County, South Carolina, and as far east as McDowell County, North Carolina (Figure 2).

Concentrations of cultural debris cover areas ranging in size from about ¼ acre to as much as 6 acres. The smaller sites could represent seasonal or special-function (e.g., hunting or mica mining) camps, or

1. Pisgah occupations were identified primarily by ceramics, which are discussed in detail in Ch. 5.

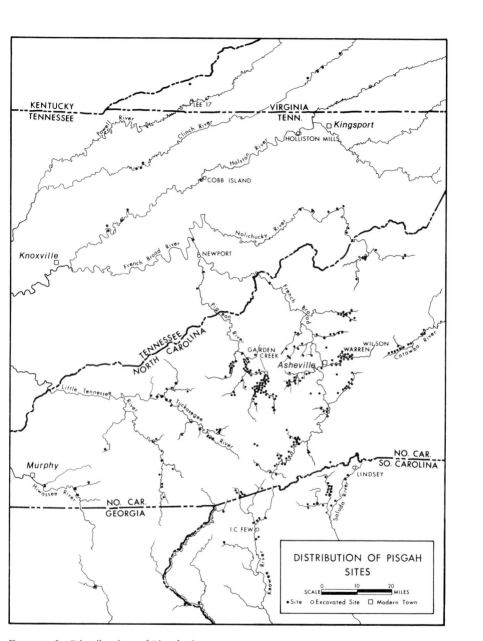

FIGURE 2. Distribution of Pisgah sites.

small groups of homesteads associated with larger villages. Specific interpretations of these smaller sites, however, will have to await further study. Nucleated villages of 2 or 3 acres in extent seem to be the most common type of settlement. Mounds, when present, are associated with large village middens.

Pisgah sites are always found in stream valleys, usually on first or second alluvial terraces. In the French Broad drainage, where comprehensive survey data are available, the sites are commonly found on the upper reaches of tributary streams, such as the Swannanoa River. In these areas, the alluvial bottomlands are more spacious than on the lower ends of the tributaries and most of the main course of the upper French Broad itself.

The Warren Wilson site is probably characteristic of a medium-sized Pisgah village. The archaeological work here was carried out slowly and systematically, and to date, it has produced the largest body of information on domestic aspects of the Pisgah cultural system.[2] This site was chosen for excavation not only because of its rich Pisgah component, but also because of its stratified remains of earlier Woodland and Archaic occupations. Consequently, about half of each season was devoted to excavations below the level of the Pisgah component, and after three summers of work, only 12,400 square feet of the Pisgah village had been exposed.

Garden Creek, the second major site discussed here, is a large and complex site, with three mounds and at least two extensive village middens. The mounds, especially, have provided information about the ceremonial and civic aspects of the Pisgah cultural system. Excavations were conducted during three field seasons, 1965-1967, and because portions of the site were under cultivation and other portions were being developed for suburban housing, only selected areas could be investigated.[3]

The procedural strategies and techniques of excavation at the two sites were relatively traditional, but were applied rigorously and with a high degree of precision. As a result, analyses could be carried out rapidly and in an orderly fashion, comparisons between sites could be made with reliability, and interpretations could be built upon firm foundations.

2. I was field supervisor at this site during the 1966, 1967, and 1968 seasons.
3. I was not directly involved in these excavations, and have relied on the excellent records of the field supervisors and on personal communications with Joffre Coe, the project director.

WARREN WILSON SITE

The Warren Wilson site was first reported in a local archaeological survey in 1940, and was again brought to the attention of the Research Laboratories in 1961. It is located on the upper Swannanoa River in Buncombe County, North Carolina. Cultural debris is scattered over approximately 3 acres on a low alluvial terrace in the interior of a bend in the river (Figure 3; Plate 1). At this point, the river is small and swift-flowing, having just passed through a hilly region to emerge into a stretch of relatively broad alluvial bottomland. Within these bottoms, surrounded by mountainous terrain, there are several smaller Pisgah village sites and a number of other sites with remains of the Woodland and Archaic periods.

Before beginning excavations at this site, and following two separate plowings, systematic surface collections were made along a 50-foot grid. These disclosed several concentrations of cultural debris, presumed to be locations of pits or house floors disturbed by the plowing. In the winter of 1965, the site was mapped and a 10-foot test square was dug to the base of the plow zone in the area of one of the debris concentrations. This test exposed a distinct line of post molds.

More extensive excavations were begun in the summer of 1966, with the objective of obtaining information on the depth and areal limits of the cultural remains. Deep testing soon revealed that the site was composed of naturally stratified sands and clays containing cultural remains to a depth of about 4 feet. Stripping of the plow zone over an area of about 2,000 square feet exposed, by the end of the summer, the post mold patterns of two houses and portions of at least three different palisade lines (Plate 2). Unfortunately, however, this work also showed that because of modern plowing and erosion, very little of the surface of the Pisgah phase village remained intact.

A typical stratigraphic profile at the site (Plate 3) exposed, from top to bottom, the following cultural zones.[4] There was an overlying plow zone (Zone A), about 1 foot thick, which contained an abundance of Pisgah remains but also some remains of earlier Connestee, Pigeon, and Swannanoa occupations. This zone was dark in color and rich in organic debris. At the base of the plow zone there was an abrupt transition to a tan-colored sandy loam (Zone B),

---

4. For a detailed description of the soil profile see Keel 1972:220-222.

PLATE 1. View of the Warren Wilson site facing south. At the time of this photograph, excavations were in the third season.

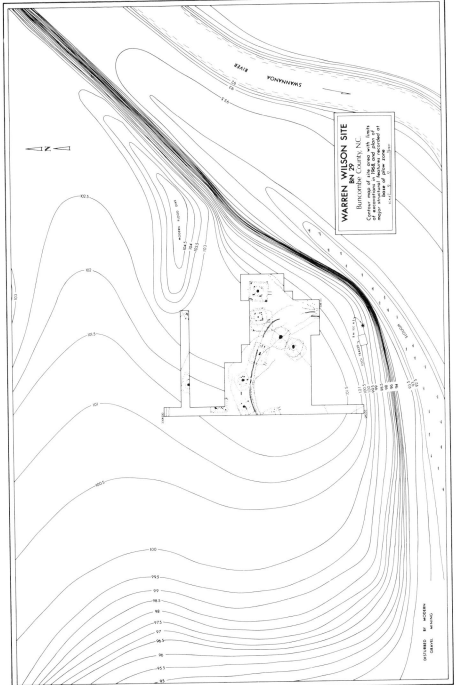

FIGURE 3. Warren Wilson site, contour map of site area.

PLATE 2. Warren Wilson excavations at the close of the first season. The area to the right is excavated only to the base of Zone A, to expose a portion of the Pisgah village pattern. To the left, a trench has been dug to the base of Zone C. A deep stratigraphic test is at the lower left.

PLATE 3. Soil profile at the Warren Wilson site. The feature at the right is inclusive in Zone C.

which was approximately ½ foot thick. Zone B contained undisturbed remains of the Swannanoa phase, including broken pottery vessels, chipping debris, and hearths, but there were also numerous pits and post molds cutting through it from the overlying Pisgah phase occupation. Zone C, about 1 foot thick, was composed of brown sandy loam with some organic content. Within this stratum were the remains of the Savannah River phase, which included a number of irregular rock clusters and rock-lined pits. Intrusive features from the Pisgah phase occupation usually extended no deeper than Zone C. Zone D, a 1-foot-thick deposit of yellowish-brown clay loam, contained the oldest cultural remains on the site. These consisted of scattered chipped stone artifacts of the Morrow Mountain phase. Below this, the soil graded from clay loam to clay films with an increase in weathered rock, presumably ancient river gravel. These clays and gravels, labeled Zones E, F, and G, were culturally sterile.

Horizontal excavation was carried out along a 10-foot grid (Plate 4). The plow zone was removed in two levels and sifted through ½-inch-mesh screens (Plate 5). Removal of the plowed soil in this manner, as opposed to stripping it with mechanized equipment, resulted in minimal destruction to shallow features and in the recovery of a more comprehensive sample of Pisgah artifacts.

When the plow zone had been completely removed from a 10-foot square, the surface (top of Zone B) was carefully troweled and all cultural features were recorded. Photographs were taken in black and white and color from a tower at an angle of about 25° from vertical. Drawings were then made on grid paper at a scale of 1 inch to 1 foot (Plate 6). As the excavations progressed, the records from each square were transferred to a master plot sheet (Figure 4).

Selected areas on the site were excavated to deeper levels in order to expose portions of the Woodland and Archaic zones (Plate 7). This aspect of the work at the Warren Wilson site is described in some detail by Keel (1972:213-279). Squares not excavated below the base of the plow zone were covered with black plastic and backfilled at the end of each season. Large features, such as burial pits, refuse pits, and hearths, were always excavated, even if the remainder of the square was not taken deeper, since they contained the only undisturbed, temporally associated assemblages of Pisgah remains.

By the end of the 1968 season, 11 different house patterns, 12 partial palisade lines, and 33 features had been assigned to the Pisgah

PLATE 4. Exploratory trench across the north portion of the Warren Wilson site, excavated during the 1968 season.

PLATE 5. Excavation of a 10-foot square at the Warren Wilson site. The plow zone soil is being sifted at the right.

PLATE 6. Students recording post molds at the base of the plow zone at the Warren Wilson site.

PLATE 7. Students excavating Swannanoa phase hearths in Zone B at the Warren Wilson site.

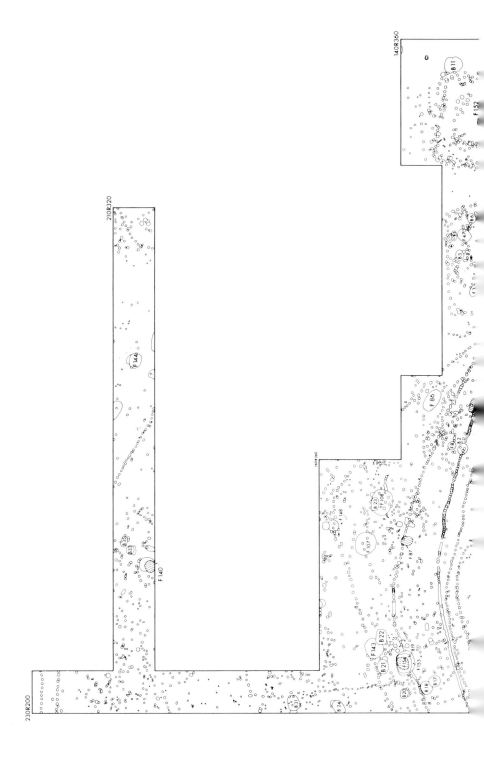

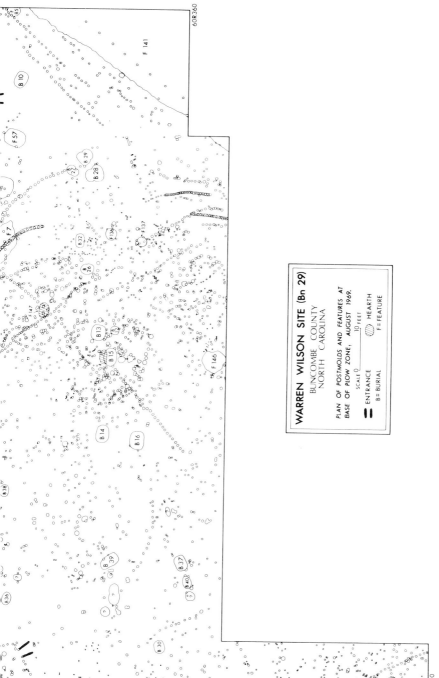

WARREN WILSON SITE (Bn 29)
BUNCOMBE COUNTY
NORTH CAROLINA

PLAN OF POSTMOLDS AND FEATURES AT
BASE OF PLOW ZONE, AUGUST 1969.

SCALE 0   10 FEET

ENTRANCE   HEARTH
B = BURIAL   F = FEATURE

FIGURE 4. Warren Wilson site, plan of post molds and features.

occupation (Figures 4, 5). Four of the house patterns were completely excavated, while seven others were only partly exposed. Other possible structures were represented by concentrations or partial alignments of post molds, even though complete patterns could not be defined. For all but one house, the floors had been cut away by modern plowing and erosion. There were many post molds of random, or seemingly random, distribution. Some of these probably were from storage cribs, sweat houses, privacy fences, skinning racks, ball posts, or any number of constructions known to have been present on sites of the Southeastern Indians in the historic period (e.g., descriptions by Bartram 1791 and Timberlake 1765).

In recording post molds, features, and burials, an attempt was always made to note intrusions or superpositioning. Sometimes, this resulted in the establishment of temporal relationships for palisades, houses, and house rebuildings. Numerous post molds (and some features) probably went unrecognized or were lost altogether to erosion, but in some instances it was possible to determine the nature of destroyed features from evidence in the overlying plow zone. For example, fragments of burnt clay might be found in the area where there had once been a hearth, and concentrations of cultural refuse usually were present in the plow zone over house patterns or along the routes of palisades, evidence of plowed-out floors and middens.

A portion of the site uncovered in 1969,[5] south and west of the major concentration of house patterns and toward the presumed center of the area enclosed by several of the palisades, had a lower density of post molds and features than previously excavated portions (Figures 4, 5). This area may represent a "plaza." More work, however, is needed to substantiate this interpretation and to determine the extent of the area and whether it contained ceremonial or civic structures.

HOUSES

Houses at the Warren Wilson site were constructed of vertical posts that were set individually in the ground, except for the vestibule entrances where they were set close together in short trenches. The buildings were square or slightly rectangular in plan, with an average measurement along the outer walls of about 20 feet. The roofs were supported by four large posts set on the house floor at

_____

5. I am grateful to Jefferson Reid and Veletta Canouts, field supervisors of the 1969 excavations, for this information.

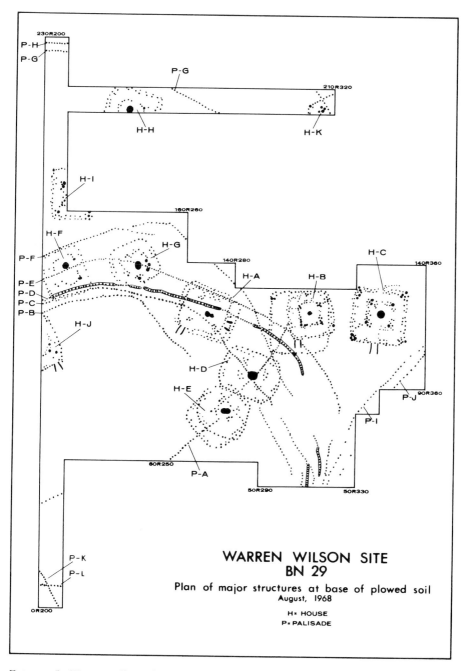

FIGURE 5. Warren Wilson site, plan of major structures.

points equidistant from the outer walls. In some cases, there was evidence that posts had been arranged between the roof supports in an effort to divide the interior of the house into rooms.

There was always evidence of replacement and addition of posts; in several instances, houses were completely rebuilt on the same locations as the previous structures. It appears that the floors were slightly lower than the surrounding ground and that there was a clay platform hearth at the center of each house. Various features, including burial pits and clay borrow pits, were found on the house floors and just outside of the houses.

Except for fragments of charred or partly decayed wall posts and occasional bits of bark or cane in pit fill, there was little direct evidence of building materials. Clay plaster, or "daub," common on many late prehistoric sites in the Southeast, was not present. Some other wall covering, possibly split-cane mats or bark, must have been used. The use of bark as a roof covering is amply documented for the Appalachian Summit region in the early historic period (Bartram 1791:296; Dickens 1967b:35). There is also the possibility that the roofs were covered with straw thatch.

House A (Figure 6):

House A was rebuilt completely at least once, as evidenced by two superimposed post mold patterns having roughly the same orientation. House A^1 was rectangular in plan, measuring 20 feet from northeast to southwest and 24 feet from northwest to southeast, with the corners slightly rounded. A pair of parallel entrance wall trenches, about 3 feet in length, extended out from the west corner of the southwest wall. Patches of burnt clay were found in the floor area, but they could not be assigned specifically to one of the building phases. Burial 1 lay directly under the burnt clay near the center of the floor. Feature 8, a shallow circular pit, also was located in the northwest portion of the floor areas of both building phases.

The northern and western walls of House A^2 lay outside of those of House A^1. The assignment of A^2 to a later date than A^1 was made on the basis of the superposition of post molds where the walls of the two structures crossed. In addition, Burial 4, which was within the wall of House A^2, cut through and obliterated a portion of the southeast wall of A^1. Since the orientation of the walls of both structures was nearly identical, it might be logically concluded that A^2 was a rebuilding of A^1 and was not just a chance intrusion of an unrelated structure. House A^2 measured approximately 20 feet from northeast to southwest and 22 feet from northwest to southeast. It, too, had slightly rounded corners. A pair of entrance trenches, 2.5 feet long, protruded from the middle of the

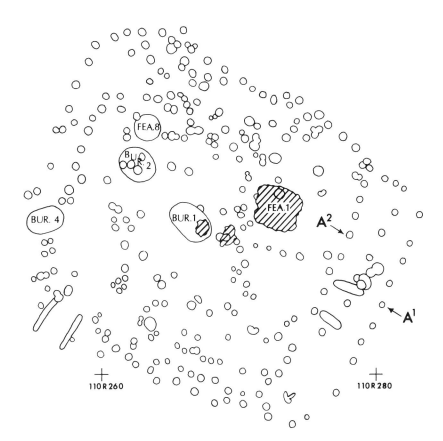

HOUSE A
(A¹ and A²)

FIGURE 6. House A at the Warren Wilson site.

southeast wall. A hearth remnant, Feature 1, was located a few feet northeast of the center of the floor. It consisted of a mass of burnt clay, measuring 3.2 x 2.9 feet across and 0.6 foot thick, which was considerably disturbed by modern plowing.

Post molds along the outer walls of both House A^1 and House A^2 measured from 0.4 to 0.7 foot in diameter (about 0.5-foot average) and from 0.2 to 1.4 feet (0.6-foot average) deeper than the modern plow zone. They all were vertical. Several larger post molds located on the floor area, possibly the remains of interior roof supports of both structures, measured from 0.7 to 0.8 foot in diameter (0.8-foot average) and from 0.6 to 1.2 feet in depth (0.8-foot average). Rocks found in several of these post molds probably served as wedges around the posts. Because the post molds of Houses A^1 and A^2 overlapped those of palisades C, D, and E, the exact patterns of inner roof supports, or of other possible interior structural features, could not be discerned.

At the extreme northwest corner of House A^2, a small area of depressed house floor was preserved below the base of plow disturbance. This was only about 0.4 foot deep at its deepest point. When troweled out, it was found to contain a fairly rich midden, but there was no hard-packed surface at the bottom. In fact, it would have been difficult to detect this depression had it not been for the profile along the 130 line (Figure 7).

House B (Figures 5, 8):

House B, like House A, showed evidence of one complete rebuilding. House B^1, the earlier structure, was about 24.5 feet square. No entrance trenches could be discerned, but the configuration of the south wall was confused by Palisade D and Feature 7. There were no remains of a hearth, but erosion and plowing had cut deeply in this area and any such feature probably would have been obliterated.

Two basin-shaped pits (Features 3 and 4), probably borrow pits for clay, were located in the northwestern portion of House B^1 and were cut through by post molds of the west wall of House B^2. Both of these pits contained small amounts of household refuse. Another small pit, Feature 37, was located in the southwestern part of this house. Hard-packed lenses of burnt sand and ash on the bottom of this pit indicate that it might have served as a secondary hearth or a small pottery kiln. Feature 53, another refuse-filled pit, was located within the southeast corner of House B^1. Post molds of the outer wall of House B^2 cut through the fill of this pit. In turn, Feature 53 was intrusive to Burial 8, which also can be attributed to House B^1. Feature 54, a large, oval, basin-shaped pit, overlapped the southeast corner of House B^1. Since this pit cut through several of the outer wall post molds of House B^1, it probably was associated with House B^2.

Post molds on the outer walls of House B^1 measured from 0.3 to 0.7

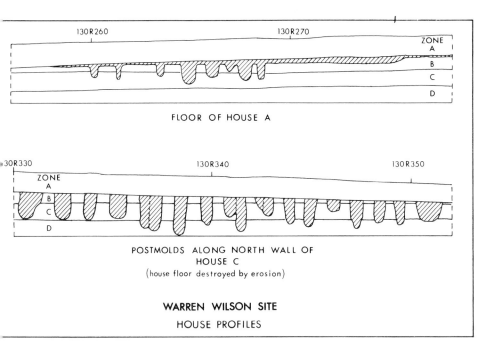

FLOOR OF HOUSE A

POSTMOLDS ALONG NORTH WALL OF
HOUSE C
(house floor destroyed by erosion)

WARREN WILSON SITE

HOUSE PROFILES

FIGURE 7. Warren Wilson site, house profiles.

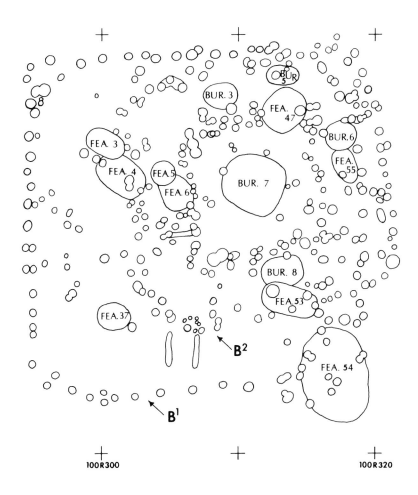

HOUSE   B
(B¹ and B²)

FIGURE 8. House B at the Warren Wilson site.

foot in diameter (0.5-foot average) and 0.3 to 0.7 foot deep (0.5-foot average). They were all vertical. Two adjoining molds at the northwest corner of the outer wall measured 0.8 foot in diameter each and were 0.7 and 0.9 foot in depth, respectively. Two similarly placed molds at the northeast corner measured 0.7 and 0.5 foot in diameter and 0.6 and 0.6 foot deep, respectively. Interior roof support post molds could not be detected. It is quite probable that they were obliterated by the extensive pit digging on the floor of House B^2.

The walls of House B^2 were similarly oriented to those of B^1. B^2 was a somewhat smaller structure, however, and it overlapped B^1 slightly on the east side. The outer walls measured approximately 18 feet square, and an inner pattern of roof supports was easily defined. A pair of entrance wall trenches protruded from the southwest corner of the south wall and were 2.5 feet in length. There was no clearly definable hearth, but chunks of burnt clay were found in the upper portion of the fill of Burial 7.

Burial 7 was located at the center of House B^2. It consisted of a deep side-chambered pit that contained the remains of a middle-aged male wearing columella bead bracelets and having an elaborate ceremonial cache and an array of mica ornamentation. Burials 3 and 5, both of which were simple pit interments of infants, were found on the north side of the structure, and Burial 6, a shaft-and-chamber interment of an infant, was found on the east side. Several refuse-filled pits, Features 5, 6, 47, and 55, were located within the wall limits of House B^2, but none of them could be assigned to B^2 with any greater certainty than to B^1.

Since House B^2 was the later of the two structures, the outer and inner wall patterns could be defined more clearly. Post molds along the outer walls were from 0.4 to 0.6 foot in diameter (0.5-foot average) and from 0.4 to 1.2 feet deep (0.7-foot average). Post molds at the corners had somewhat wider and deeper dimensions. At the northwest corner two post molds measured 0.7 and 0.6 foot across and 1.2 and 1.1 feet deep, respectively. At the southwest corner a single post mold measured 1.1 feet in diameter and 1.5 feet deep. And at the southeast corner a single post mold measured 1.1 feet in diameter and 1 foot deep.

Interior roof supports were indicated by large post molds located about 4 feet in from each corner of the outer wall. The northwest roof support was represented by a post mold that measured 0.9 foot in diameter and 1.3 feet deep. The northeast post mold measured 1.1 feet across and was 1.4 feet deep. Two adjoining southwest post molds (evidence of either reinforcement or replacement of the post at that corner) measured 0.9 and 1.1 feet in diameter and 1.1 and 1.1 feet deep, respectively. And at the southeast juncture there were two post molds, one of which was 0.7 foot in diameter and 1.7 feet deep, and the other 0.8 foot in diameter and 1.4 feet deep.

Smaller posts aligned between the roof supports formed a central enclosure about 10 feet square. In size and depth, these post molds were duplicates of those along the outer walls. Rocks had been wedged around several of the larger post molds on both the inner and the outer walls. All of the post molds were vertical, except for the northeast corner post which slanted inward from the top toward the center of the structure.

House C (Figures 5, 9; Plate 8):

House C appears to have been constructed somewhat more symmetrically than others described thus far. The clarity with which the pattern was defined, however, was at least partly due to the absence of earlier or later patterns in the same area. This house obviously saw considerable post reinforcement and replacement along both the inner and the outer walls, but there was no indication of total rebuilding as with Houses A and B. The structure measured 22 feet square, and the corners were slightly rounded. A pattern of post molds for an inner wall connecting the interior roof supports lay 5 feet in from the outer walls and enclosed an area approximately 12 feet square. The bottom portion of a basin-shaped clay hearth (Feature 152) was encountered at the exact center of the structure, and pieces of fired clay were found at the same location in the overlying plow zone. A pair of entrance wall trenches 4 feet long and 2 feet apart protruded from the center of the south wall. A single shallow post mold, which was located exactly between the trenches and in line with the wall, probably served as a retainer for a doorstop. A gap in the post mold pattern along the north wall may represent a back entrance to the house, and a row of eight posts aligned roughly parallel to the back wall might have served as a windscreen across that opening.

Burial 9 was the only disturbance on the floor of House C. Burial 11 was found at the northeast corner, but since posts of the outer house wall intruded through the burial pit fill, the burial was probably of an earlier date than the house. Burial 10 was located 7 feet to the south of House C, and whether or not it was related to the structure is indeterminable. A large shallow depression (Feature 57) filled with ash, charcoal, bone, pottery, and other refuse was located 8 feet to the southwest of House C. This feature could have resulted from the occupation of either House B or House C, or from neither.

Erosional damage was greatest at the southeast corner of House C. Consequently, post molds were very shallow in that area and a few probably were lost in the process of troweling after the plow zone had been removed. This may explain the thicker distribution of posts along the west and north walls. It would appear that House C, as in the case of B^2, was divided into separate rooms by the erection of posts between the four interior roof supports. These additional posts probably helped also to support the horizontal roof beams. It would appear that openings

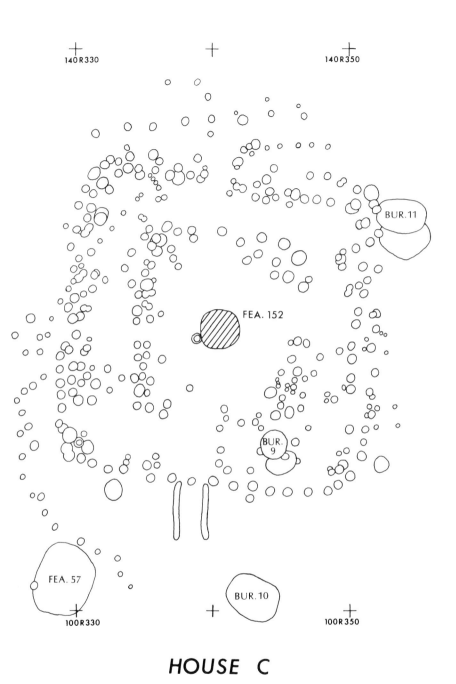

140R330

140R350

BUR.11

FEA. 152

BUR.
9

FEA. 57

BUR.10

100R330

100R350

HOUSE C

FIGURE 9. House C at the Warren Wilson site.

PLATE 8. House C at the Warren Wilson site after excavation of pits and post molds. The view is to the north.

were left in each of these interior walls, the widest of these being on the south wall opposite the entrance.

Post molds on the west outer wall, where erosion had cut less deeply, were from 0.4 to 0.7 foot in diameter (0.6-foot average) and from 0.5 to 1.7 feet deep (1.1-feet average). Larger and deeper posts again were found at the corners of the outer walls. At the northwest corner there was a cluster of three large posts measuring 1.4, 0.8, and 1.2 feet in diameter and 1.3, 1.3, and 1.8 feet in depth, respectively. At the northeast corner a single large post was 1.2 feet across and 0.8 foot deep; at the southwest corner two post molds measured 1 foot and 0.9 foot in diameter and 1.2 feet and 1 foot deep, respectively; and at the eroded southeast corner, the largest post was 0.7 foot across and 0.8 foot deep. There were four large interior roof supports. The one on the northwest was 0.8 foot in diameter and 1.5 feet deep, the one on the northeast was 0.9 foot across and 0.9 foot deep, the one on the southwest was 1.1 feet across and 1.3 feet deep, and the one on the southeast was 0.8 foot in diameter and 2.3 feet deep. Several of the corner post molds on the outer wall were slanted inward toward the center of the structure. The deeply set southeast roof support also slanted inward. Selected post mold profiles from House C are provided in Figure 7.

House D (Figure 5):

Other house patterns have been recognized in the area thus far excavated, but their dimensions and structural details are less well defined than for Houses A, B, and C. In some cases this resulted from the confusion created by several post mold patterns intersecting (as in the case of House F, which overlay four earlier palisade lines); at other times it is because the current excavations have exposed only a portion of the pattern. House D was located just to the south of Houses A and B. The pattern was roughly rectangular, with the short walls bulging slightly. The outer walls measured 18 feet from northeast to southwest and about 25 feet from northwest to southeast. Interior roof supports were located at points 8 feet in from the northwest and southeast walls and 6 feet in from the northeast and southwest walls. The plow-disturbed remnant of a baked-clay hearth (Feature 147) was found at the center of the structure. No entrance wall trenches were discovered, and no other form of entrance area was discernible. There were no pits or burials in the floor area of this structure, although Burials 26 and 32 were located just outside of the southeast corner. This house pattern overlay portions of Palisades A, C, and F.

House E (Figure 5):

House E was represented by a concentration of post molds immediately to the southwest of House D. At least two separate structures, probably a rebuilding sequence as with Houses A and B, were indicated. Possibly the pattern located slightly farther to the southwest and oriented more in a northeast-southwest direction was the earlier of the two, and it was designated House E^1. Both patterns overlay a section of Palisade A. House E^1 measured approximately 20 feet northwest to southeast and 17 feet northeast to southwest. The locations of interior posts could not be determined, and there was no evidence of an entrance or hearth. House E^2, the second and possibly later pattern, overlapped House E^1 on the north and east sides. House E^2 appears to have been about 18 feet square, with rounded corners. Two adults (Burials 13 and 15) and an infant (Burial 12) were buried in the floor. Burial 15, located at the center of the structure, was partially covered by the remains of a baked-clay hearth, and burnt clay, charred wood, and ash were generously distributed through the upper portion of the burial fill. Four large post molds, located about 5 feet in from each corner of the structure, marked the location of interior roof supports for this house. Burials 14 and 16 were located just outside of the House E complex.

House F (Figure 5):

The east and west outer walls of House F were easily defined, but the north and south walls were difficult to distinguish because they coincided with portions of Palisades C and F. The house pattern was roughly 18 feet square and was oriented northwest-southeast. There was no clearly defined entrance. It was possible to pick out several interior post molds, but these were distinctly defined only on the east side where they were located about 4 feet in from the outer wall.

On the north-central floor area of House F, a partially intact clay hearth (Feature 154) was uncovered within a large shallow pit (Feature 153). On excavating the pit, it was found that the hearth overlay a burial pit (Burial 19). The pit fill around the hearth and in the topmost fill of the burial pit contained chunks of burnt clay and charred wood. It is probable that an old hearth had been removed by the digging of Feature 153, after which the burial had been made and a new hearth, Feature 154, constructed over it (Figure 11; Plate 18). Five other burials (Burials 17, 18, 20, 21, and 22) were found in the floor area of House F. Burial 22 intruded through a large, shallow, refuse-filled pit (Feature 143).

Post molds and pits of House F were superimposed on four palisade lines. The south wall posts overlapped posts of Palisades C and D. Features 153 and 154 and Burials 18 and 19 overlay Palisade E. Burial 21 and Feature 143, as well as post molds from the north wall of the house, intruded on Palisade F.

House G:

The post mold pattern for House G was indistinct, but it probably conformed in size and orientation to House F (Figure 5). The remains of a baked-clay hearth (Feature 87) were encountered at the approximate center of the structure, and there were two large refuse-filled pits (Features 107 and 108) just to the north and northeast of this hearth. Feature 108 contained a small burial pit with the remains of a young female. House G is believed to postdate Palisade E since Feature 87 seemed to cut through several post molds of that palisade.

House H:

House H was partially uncovered in 1968, during the excavation of the east-west trench along the 200 line (Figure 5). This structure appears to be oriented northeast-southwest, possibly in alignment with Palisade G. Only parts of the northwest, northeast, and southeast walls were exposed. From northwest to southeast the structure measured approximately 20 feet, and northern and western interior post molds were found at points 5 feet in from the outer walls. A clay fire basin (Feature 140) was located at what probably was the center of this structure. Beneath this hearth was the shaft-and-chamber burial of an adult (Burial 33). Two other burials (Burials 34 and 35) were found within the wall pattern.

House I:

House I was defined by a post mold pattern that was partially uncovered in 1968 (Figure 5). The west and south walls were fully exposed, but all of the east wall and most of the north wall remained unexcavated. This house was oriented north-south by east-west. The pattern measured 20 feet along the west wall and about 17 feet along the south wall. Interior posts were clearly indicated in a line about 5 feet in from the west wall. There were no pits on the exposed floor area; however, Burial 31 lay just outside of the west wall and Burial 24 was located near the southwest corner.

House J:

Another house pattern was partially exposed in the north-south trench and was designated House J (Figure 5). The entire east wall and a portion of the south wall were exposed. The structure faced southeast and was aligned with the palisades found immediately to the north. The east wall was 19 feet long, and the corners were slightly rounded. Entrance trenches were present at the southeast corner of the south wall. Several large post molds marked the position of the southeast interior roof support, and a single burial (Burial 25) was found in the southeast corner of the floor just behind the entrance.

House K:

House K was represented only by the northwest corner of a possible wall pattern found in the easternmost extension of the east-west trench (Figure 5). Approximately 5 feet in from the corner was a cluster of large post molds that probably marked the location of the structure's northwest interior roof support. A portion of a palisade line, possibly Palisade

H, crossed this pattern, but the temporal priority of the two constructions could not be determined.

PALISADES

Twelve linear post mold patterns, usually having slightly larger
and more closely spaced posts than the houses, were interpreted as
palisades. One of these had the posts set in a trench, whereas the
others appear to have had the posts set individually. Several of the
patterns were only exposed for short distances, and the classification of these as palisades is tentative. Also, some of these short segments will probably turn out to be different parts of the same palisade. It has been suggested that such palisades served as fortifica-
tions, which were necessitated by competition for arable lands
among the late prehistoric Southeastern Indians (Larson 1972:383-
392).

Palisade A:
    Palisade A was represented by a line of post molds running in a northeast-
    southwest direction across the central part of the excavated area (Figure
    5). Although five other patterns, Palisades B, C, D, E, and F, crossed this
    line in a perpendicular fashion, only Palisades D and F were definitely in-
    trusive through Palisade A. However, since F was intrusive through E and
    D, it could be concluded that D, E, and F were all of more recent con-
    struction than A. Houses B, D, and E also appear to overlie Palisade A.
    Palisade A had a distinct offset of about 4 feet at the location where it
    was overlain by House E.

Palisade B:
    Palisade B was located in the central portion of the excavation (Figure 5;
    Plate 9). It ran for about 40 feet from southwest to northeast and then
    turned rather abruptly to the southeast. It was traced for another 100
    feet, except where Houses D and E intruded. It conformed in general to
    the alignments of Palisades C, D, E, and F. If it can be assumed that these
    enclosures were built in a sequence of expansions of the village, then Pali-
    sade B would represent the oldest of the five constructions.

Palisade C:
    Palisade C lay just outside of Palisade B (Figure 5; Plate 9). It conformed
    generally to the directions taken by Palisade B, having at first a south-
    west-to-northeast orientation, after which it turned in a meandering
    curve to the southeast. Finally, in the south end of the excavation, the
    pattern seemed to turn back to the southwest. At this point, there was a
    4-foot offset in the pattern, which may represent an entrance. Palisade C
    was overlain by Palisade D and by houses D, E, F, and G.

PLATE 9. Portions of Palisades B and C at the Warren Wilson site.

Palisade D:

Palisade D lay just outside of Palisade C and conformed in general to the direction taken by both B and C (Figure 5). It was intersected by two later house patterns, Houses A and B. This palisade differed from the others on the site in that the posts were set in a deep trench (Plate 10). A long shallow depression (Feature 7), containing a dense concentration of charcoal, animal bone, pottery, and other village debris, was associated with a portion of this trench (Figure 4). An overlapping offset in the trench near the south end of the excavation may represent an entrance.

The trench was lost for a distance of about 25 feet along the east side, but it was rediscovered in the southern end of the excavation. This missing section is difficult to explain, since the trench was rather deep at the point where it abruptly ended in square 90R310. However, just below the plow zone at this location a large, thickly clustered group of stones was uncovered which was determined to be the remains of a Swannanoa phase hearth. The palisade trench ended at the northwest edge of these stones, and it is conceivable that as the trench was being dug, the subsurface rocks of the buried hearth were encountered and that for the next 25 feet the posts were set in the ground individually at shallower depths. The molds of these shallower posts might then have been lost to erosion as were parts of other palisade patterns in this more eroded part of the site.

Palisade E:

Palisade E lay several feet outside of Palisade D and was of similar orientation (Figure 5), but the posts were set in individual holes. Approximately 200 feet of this palisade was uncovered. It was intersected by four later house patterns, Houses A, B, F, and G.

Palisade F:

Palisade F was represented by a line of post molds that ran from a point on the western extremity of the excavations, along a line northeastward, approximately to grid point 155R250 where it turned rather sharply to the southeast (Figure 5). As it proceeded southeastward, it crossed, in turn, Palisades E, D, and A. The pattern was lost in the eroded area southeast of House D.

Two parallel rows of post molds that crossed the northern end of the north-south exploration trench were interpreted as being segments of palisade lines (Figure 5). The southernmost of these was labeled Palisade G, and the northernmost was designated Palisade H. These lay some 80 feet north of Palisade F. A continuation of Palisade G is believed to be present in a row of post molds running diagonally across the central portion of the east-west exploration trench (Figure 5).

Palisades I and J:

Palisades I and J were represented by parallel rows of post molds on the

PLATE 10. Excavated section of Palisade D at the Warren Wilson site.

GARDNER-WEBB COLLEGE LIBRARY
P. O. Box 836
Boiling Springs, N.C. 28017

eastern periphery of the excavated area along the bank of the slough bordering the river (Figure 5). At the close of the 1968 season, a midden deposit (Feature 141) was encountered on the slope of the bank just outside of Palisades I and J. Additional excavation in this area in 1969 revealed that the midden was present in a continuing belt along the outside of the palisade lines (Figure 4) and that it sloped in the direction of the river and had a maximum depth of about 5 feet.

Palisades K and L:
    Two possible palisade patterns, designated Palisades K and L, were discovered in the south end of the north-south exploratory trench (Figure 5). Palisade K was aligned northwest-southeast, and Palisade L was aligned west-east.

As noted earlier, Palisades D, E, and F all were more recent than Palisade A. It also could be determined, on the basis of the superposition of intersecting post molds, that F was more recent than D and E and that D was more recent than C. By assuming that the construction of each of these palisades represents successive enlargements of the village, it may be postulated that the sequence from oldest to youngest is A, B, C, D, E, and F. Having uncovered such limited portions of Palisades G, H, I, J, and K, it was not possible to interpret their temporal relationships one to another or to the other palisades. However since Houses A, B, D, E, F, and G were found to overlie one or more of the palisades in group A to F, it must be concluded that these houses were surrounded by one or more larger enclosures. Palisades G, H, or K could be parts of such enclosures.

By assuming that the topography of the site has not been greatly altered in modern times (although there certainly have been some changes), and that in spite of the meandering character of the patterns there was some degree of overall symmetry, an attempt can be made to project the missing portions of the palisades. In the instance of Palisade E, by projecting an equal amount of curve on the south side as was found on the north side, and then by completing the pattern to form an irregular circle (bringing it just to the edge of the steep bank on the south), an approximate plan of the complete enclosure can be obtained. It would have measured about 150 to 180 feet on each side and contained a total area of around 22,000 to 32,000 square feet. Palisades A, B, C, and D probably would have enclosed slightly smaller areas, whereas F would have been larger and perhaps more rectangular in shape. Offsets in Palisades A and D appear to have formed entrances on the southeast side facing the river.

Overall dimensions and shapes of the larger enclosures, indicated by the patterns labeled Palisades G, H, I, J, K, and L, cannot even be estimated. However, from the indications of upturned charcoal, burnt clay, and other village debris, the total habitation area covered about 100,000 to 150,000 square feet, or about 3 acres. This is roughly the area bounded on the east, south, and west by the 100-foot contour line and on the north by the long depression at about where the contour intervals are marked on Figure 3. One should not conclude from this that all 3 acres were enclosed and occupied at a single moment in time, since rather than simply expanding concentrically, the village may have shifted to some extent during its development.

FEATURES

A feature designation was placed on such remains as borrow pits, storage pits, midden deposits, hearths, house entrance trenches, and individually excavated segments of palisades. Most of these features had some amount of associated refuse—artifacts, heat-fractured rock, charcoal, ash, food remains, etc. Some features contained large amounts of deposited garbage, while others contained only a scattering of incidental materials. When the pit fill contained recognizable organic refuse, all of the soil was carried to the laboratory where it was subjected to fine screening and flotation, through which microremains (seeds, nutshells, maize kernels, small bones, fish scales, small flint chips, beads, etc.) were recovered. Numbers assigned to the following Pisgah features are not consecutive because work was often carried out simultaneously on several stratigraphic levels on the site, which resulted in some numbers being assigned to features of the other cultural components.

Feature 1:

Feature 1 was a low platform of burnt clay located at the approximate center of House A^2 (Figure 6). It was interpreted as the central fireplace of that structure. Although heavily damaged by modern plowing, a semblance of its original form remained. It measured 3.2 x 2.9 feet across the top and was 0.6 foot thick.

Feature 3:

Feature 3 (Figure 10; Plate 11) was one of several relatively shallow pits found on the floors of Houses B^1 and B^2. It measured 2.8 x 2 feet across the top and 1.5 feet deep, and the sides sloped inward toward the bottom. It was intersected by post molds of the west wall of House B^2 and, there-

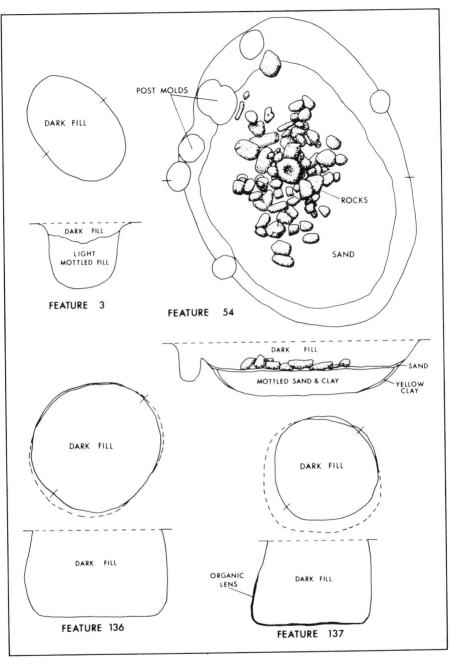

FIGURE 10. Features 3, 54, 136, and 137 at the Warren Wilson site.

PLATE 11. Feature 3 at the Warren Wilson site.

fore, was considered to be associated with House B^1. The upper few inches of fill in this pit contained household refuse, but the lower portion was relatively sterile. This could have been a storage pit or a borrow pit for clay, but the latter seems to be the more probable interpretation. The lower portion of the fill was sterile, which suggests that the hole was at least partly refilled soon after being dug.

Feature 4:

Feature 4 was intersected by Feature 3 and by several post molds on the west wall of House B^2. It was basin-shaped and measured 2.5 feet across the top and 2 feet deep. As with Feature 3, only the top portion of fill contained refuse. This probably was a refilled borrow pit.

Feature 5:

This was a circular basin-shaped pit, probably a clay borrow pit, on the floor of House B^2. It intersected Feature 6. It measured 1.9 feet across the top and 1.3 feet deep. The top 0.4 foot of fill was dark in color and contained cultural refuse. Below that, the fill was a light color and relatively sterile of cultural remains.

Feature 6:

This pit was intersected by Feature 5 and by several interior post molds of House B^2. It was a shallow basin-shaped pit that measured 2.5 x 2 feet across the top and 1.6 feet deep. The top 0.6 foot of fill was dark and contained refuse, whereas the bottom 1 foot was lighter in color and had only a scattering of cultural remains, indicating a refilled borrow pit.

Feature 7:

Feature 7 was a long, shallow, irregular depression (Plate 10). The overall length was 17.2 feet, and the width varied from 3.2 feet near the northwest end to 5.3 feet near the southeast end. The depth at the deepest point was 0.5 foot. This depression is believed to be associated with the trench for Palisade D. It is possible that when the villagers were digging the trench for Palisade D, one of the numerous Swannanoa phase hearths was encountered. A shallow excavation then would have been necessary to remove these stones so that the trench could be continued uninterrupted. Such an explanation would account for the numerous rocks found in the fill of this feature. Following the construction of Palisade D, the depression was backfilled with its original dirt mixed with abundant village refuse including a quantity of food remains.

Feature 8:

This was a circular pit found in the northwest floor area of House A. The feature measured 2 feet in diameter and 1.4 feet deep. The sides were straight and the bottom was flat. It might have been a clay borrow pit, unfinished burial pit, or storage pit. It contained a scattering of cultural refuse throughout the fill.

Feature 9:

Feature 9 was assigned to a section of Palisade D excavated early in the 1966 season. This portion of the trench was from 0.4 to 0.6 foot deep and contained 12 post molds. The bottoms of the individual post molds penetrated from 0.1 to 0.4 foot below the bottom of the trench.

Feature 14:

This number was assigned to another section of Palisade D in square 120R260. This section was from 0.4 to 0.6 foot deep and contained 11 identifiable post impressions in the bottom. These penetrated from 0.1 to 0.8 foot below the bottom of the trench.

Feature 37:

This was a shallow, circular, basin-shaped pit located on the southwest portion of the floor of House B^1. It intersected the edge of Feature 7. The pit measured 2 feet in diameter and was 1 foot deep at the center. The lower sides and bottom were lined with burnt sand and ash. It may have functioned as a secondary cooking pit or small pottery kiln for House B^1.

Feature 40:

This number was given to the entrance wall trenches of House A^2. The northernmost trench measured 0.8 foot wide, 2.5 feet long, and 0.6 foot deep. The southernmost trench was 0.7 foot wide, 1.4 feet long, and 0.6 foot deep. Post impressions were not encountered in the bottoms of the trenches.

Feature 41:

This number was assigned to the entrance wall trenches at the southwest corner of House A^1. The westernmost trench measured 3.4 feet long, 0.5 foot wide, and 0.6 foot deep. The easternmost trench was 2.9 feet long, 0.4 foot wide, and 0.6 foot deep. There were no post impressions in the bottoms of the trenches.

Feature 47:

This was a bathtub-shaped pit in the northeast portion of House B^2. It was intersected by at least one large post mold of that structure, possibly an inner roof support. The feature measured 3.1 x 2.8 feet across the top and was 2.2 feet deep. It may have been a clay borrow pit or an unused burial pit (it conformed to the usual shape of the simple burial pit). The top 0.8 foot of the fill contained a large amount of refuse, including a quantity of charcoal, whereas the lower fill was culturally sterile.

Feature 53:

This was a rectangular pit, 4 feet long and 2 feet wide, on the floor of House B^1. It was cut through by post molds of the south wall of House B^2. The shape of the pit suggests that it was begun as a burial pit. In cleaning out the fill, the excavator found that the pit extended only to a depth of 1.1 feet, at which level a mass of large stones was encountered. These stones later proved to be a hearth of the Savannah River phase occupation. It is probable that Feature 53 was abandoned before completion because of the obstacle of the buried hearth.

Feature 54:
Feature 54 (Figure 10; Plates 12, 13) was a large oval basin located outside of the southeast corner of the post mold pattern for House B[1] and probably was associated with that structure. It measured 7 feet from northwest to southeast and 5 feet from southwest to northeast. It was 1.3 feet deep at the center. At the bottom of the plowed soil, this feature appeared as a large oval patch of dark fill mottled with yellow clay. Upon excavation, a cluster of heat-cracked river pebbles was encountered at a depth of 0.5 foot below the top of the pit (Plate 12). These stones were resting on a thin layer of white sand, which in turn overlay a layer of mottled sand and clay that extended to the bottom of the pit. The lower sides of the pit were lined with bright-yellow subsoil clay. There was a scattering of cultural refuse among the stones in the central part of the fill. Several post molds were located on the periphery of the feature, but these did not form a distinct pattern. The clay and sand layers suggest that the pit had a prepared floor, and even though the stones were heat-fractured, there was no evidence for there having been a fire in the pit itself. It is possible that this was the subsurface floor of a crude sweat house of the type described in historic accounts (Bartram 1791:296-297; Timberlake 1765:61).

Feature 55:
This was an oblong bathtub-shaped pit on the floor of House B[1]. It measured 2.6 x 1.4 across and was 0.8 foot deep. It contained a scattering of cultural refuse and probably was a clay borrow pit or an unfinished burial pit.

Feature 56:
This number was assigned to a section of Palisade D, the excavation of which was begun late in the 1966 season and completed in 1967. This section was approximately 18 feet long and from 0.6 to 1.6 feet deep. Some of the post molds extended to a depth of 1.2 feet below the bottom of the trench, while others were marked only by slight depressions of 0.05 foot or less in depth. The width of the trench varied from 0.7 to 1 foot.

Feature 57:
This was a large oval depression similar to Feature 54. It was located 8 feet from the southwest corner of House C. It measured 6 x 4.3 feet across the top and was 0.5 foot deep at the deepest point. The pit fill

PLATE 12. Feature 54 at the Warren Wilson site excavated to the sand and rock level.

PLATE 13. Feature 54 at the Warren Wilson site completely excavated.

contained an abundance of cultural refuse, including a 1.5 x 3.5 foot concentration of heat-fractured stones, ash, clay, animal bones, and charcoal.

Feature 85:
This small basin-shaped pit was on the eastern border of the excavated area. It measured 3.2 feet across the top and was 0.7 foot deep at the center. It may have functioned as a cooking pit.

Feature 86:
This was a large trough-shaped pit located a few feet north of House A (Plates 14, 15). It measured 5.8 x 3.2 feet across the top and was 1.0 foot deep at the deepest point. The fill of this pit contained a number of heat-fractured river pebbles as well as a quantity of cultural refuse.

Feature 87:
This was a small patch of burnt clay, all that remained of the central hearth of House G. It measured 2.6 x 2.2 feet across and was 0.2 foot thick. Almost all of the hearth had been removed by plowing, and there was little indication of its original form.

Feature 107:
This was a large, shallow, refuse-filled pit located at the northwest corner of House G. Three corner posts of the house cut through the pit fill, indicating that the feature predated the house. The pit measured 5.6 x 5.1 feet across the top and was 0.5 foot deep. It had straight walls and a flat floor.

Feature 108:
Feature 108 was almost identical in size and shape to Feature 107 and was located just 5 feet to the southeast. It, also, was intersected by posts of House G. The pit measured 6.3 x 5.5 feet across and was 0.6 foot deep. The sides were straight and the bottom flat. A small pit containing Burial 23 (Plate 38) was found in the floor of this feature. It could not be determined whether the burial pit had been dug before or after the excavation of the feature. It definitely had not been dug through the fill of the larger pit.

Feature 136:
This was a small circular pit located a few feet to the southeast of House D (Plate 16). It was 2.9 feet in diameter and 2 feet deep. The sides expanded near the bottom to a diameter of 3.2 feet, and the floor was flat. The floor and lower walls of the pit were hard-packed, indicating that the pit had seen a good deal of use before abandonment. The fill was homogeneously saturated with refuse from top to bottom, an obvious case of garbage disposal. This pit probably served as a storage chamber for vegetable foods, and after its abandonment it was backfilled with household waste.

PLATE 14. Feature 86 at the Warren Wilson site before excavation.

PLATE 15. Feature 86 at the Warren Wilson site completely excavated.

PLATE 16. Feature 136 at the Warren Wilson site.

Feature 137:

This pit was located 5 feet south of Feature 136 and was almost identical to it in size and shape (Figure 10). The orifice was 2.3 feet in diameter, but near the bottom it expanded to a diameter of 2.8 feet. It was 1.9 feet deep. The floor was flat, and as with Feature 136, the sides and bottom were packed hard. In this case there was a thin layer of dark organic material on the lower walls and floor. A small amount of refuse was concentrated in the top few inches of fill. This feature was also interpreted as a food storage pit. During the laboratory processing of artifacts from Features 136 and 137, it was found that sherds from both features fit together. Therefore, it may be concluded that the two features were backfilled at the same time and that they probably were in use contemporaneously.

Feature 140:

This feature number was assigned to a baked-clay hearth overlying Burial 33 (Figure 11; Plate 17). This hearth apparently had been constructed over the burial pit not long after the interment was made. When the chamber of the burial collapsed, the hearth had slumped into the top of the pit and had then become filled with refuse. The hearth was 2.6 feet in diameter and 0.3 foot thick.

Feature 141:

On the extreme southeastern limits of the 1968 excavations, a dark-colored, artifact-bearing soil was found to underlie the plow zone and to slope toward the southeast. It seemed to run parallel to the river for some distance, beginning just outside of Palisades I and J. No attempt was made to explore this feature in 1968; however, an excavation made in 1969 revealed that it was an extensive, deeply stratified deposit that had resulted from garbage disposal and natural erosion along the southeastern periphery of the village.

Features 143 and 144:

The outlines of both of these features were defined in 1968, but they were not excavated until 1969. The following descriptions were extracted from summary weekly reports compiled by one of the site supervisors (Veletta Canouts, personal communication).

Feature 143 was a shallow pit, about 5 feet in diameter. Burial 22 intruded into the southeast corner. Bone, flint, charcoal, and pottery were found throughout the fill, and a thin layer of yellow clay, mottled with dark organic soil, was encountered at the bottom of the pit (0.8 foot from the base of the plow zone). Zone C was found uniformly at the bottom of the pit. Two burials (Burials 21 and 22) were located adjacent to the pit, and these may have been the source of the yellow clay in the fill of Feature 143.

Feature 144 was located in square 200R290 and was about 3 x 4 feet

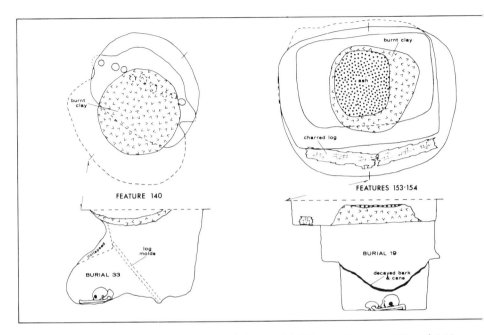

FIGURE 11. Feature 140 (overlying Burial 33) and Features 153 and 154 (overlying Burial 19) at the Warren Wilson site.

PLATE 17. Feature 140, overlying Burial 33, at the Warren Wilson site.

across the top and 0.5 foot deep. It was filled with Pisgah refuse, including pottery sherds, charcoal, animal bones, and fire-cracked rocks.

Feature 147:
This feature represented the plow-disturbed remains of a baked-clay
hearth, located at the approximate center of House D. In its original
form it probably was a low platform having a diameter of about 3 feet.

Feature 152:
This was the plow-disturbed remnant of a baked-clay hearth, located at
the center of House C (Figure 9; Plate 8). It was about 3 feet in diameter.

Features 153 and 154 (Figure 11; Plate 18):
These features were found in the central part of the floor of House F.
Feature 153 was a shallow pit that measured 5.5 feet from east to west
and 4.5 feet from north to south. Situated within this pit was a baked-
clay platform hearth, Feature 154, which was 0.6 foot thick and about
2.6 feet in diameter. In the fill of Feature 153, and surrounding the
hearth, was a quantity of burnt clay, ash, and wood, including a large section of a charred log. When the hearth was removed, the pit of Burial 19
was encountered. It is hypothesized that Feature 153 was dug for the
purpose of removing a hearth on the floor of House D so that Burial 19
could be placed under the hearth site. After the completion of the burial,
a new hearth (Feature 154) was constructed in the place of the old one.
The cavity around the new hearth was then backfilled with the burnt
clay, ash, and charred wood from the old hearth.

PLAZA

By the beginning of the 1968 season, it had become evident from
the curvature of Palisades B to F, and from the orientations of most
of the identified house patterns, that the center of the village in its
early stages was somewhat to the south of House J and to the west
of House E. An exploratory north-south trench across this area
(Plate 19) revealed a surface relatively free of post molds and other
village features.

In 1969, a 40 x 60 foot section of plow zone was stripped from
this area (Veletta Canouts, personal communication). Five burials
and three pit features were found, but post molds were much fewer
and cultural refuse in the plow zone was less dense than in areas to
the north and east. This information suggests the presence of a
"plaza" in the center of the village during at least part of its existence.

PLATE 18. Features 153 and 154, overlying Burial 19, at the Warren Wilson site.

PLATE 19. Exploratory trench across the plaza area at the Warren Wilson site. This trench was excavated during the 1968 season.

GARDEN CREEK SITE

The Garden Creek site occupies approximately 12 acres on the south side of the Pigeon River, just upstream from its juncture with Garden Creek, in Haywood County, North Carolina (Figure 1). In actuality, several roughly contiguous sites are involved (Figure 12). Mound No. 1 (labeled Hw 1 on Figure 12) is located on the northeast end of the site. It has an associated village midden that covers about 5 acres (Hw 7 on Figure 12). On slightly higher ground, about 1,000 feet west of the first mound, is situated Mound No. 2 (Hw 2 on Figure 12). This mound, first tested by a local resident for the Valentine Museum in 1880, has an adjacent 4-acre village midden (Hw 8 on Figure 12). The remnant of a third mound (Hw 3 on Figure 12), extensively excavated by the Heye Foundation in 1915, is located on the southern margins of the site. Here there is no apparent associated village midden.

All of the Research Laboratories' excavations at Garden Creek were oriented along a 5-foot grid. In the mound work, an effort was made to preserve remaining portions of floors and building stages and to avoid deep vertical cuts. In short, the techniques of excavation were aimed at dismantling the mounds in the reverse order of their construction. Necessary stratigraphic profiles were obtained at the mound margins and were carried down in successive stages as the horizontal stripping progressed. Detailed graphic records were kept on all phases of these excavations, and a 5-foot-square soil monolith was preserved at the center of each mound for future archaeological reference.

MOUNDS

From the Heye Foundation's report (Heye 1919:35-43 and Plate 2) it could be determined with reasonable certainty that Mound No. 3 (referred to by Heye as the James Plott Mound) was built in pre-Pisgah times. A layer of boulders overlying the core mound constituted the only resemblance to Pisgah mound architecture. Artifacts found in the general mound fill and in various mound and sub-mound features suggest that the mound was a product of the Connestee, or possibly even of the earlier Pigeon, occupation at Garden Creek.[6] Pottery sherds, for instance, were described as including

---

6. Keel (1972:89) suggests that this mound was built during the Pisgah occupation.

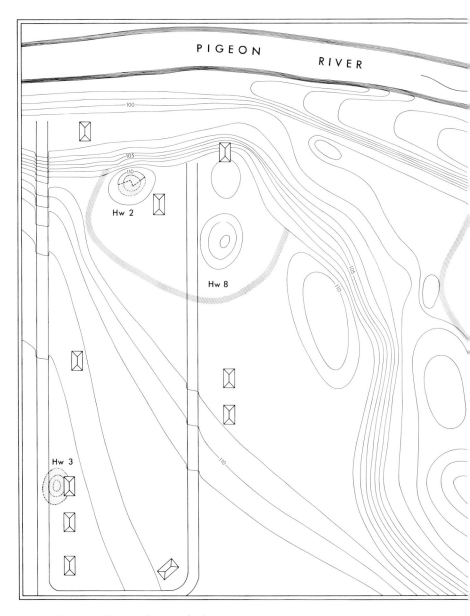

FIGURE 12. Garden Creek sites.

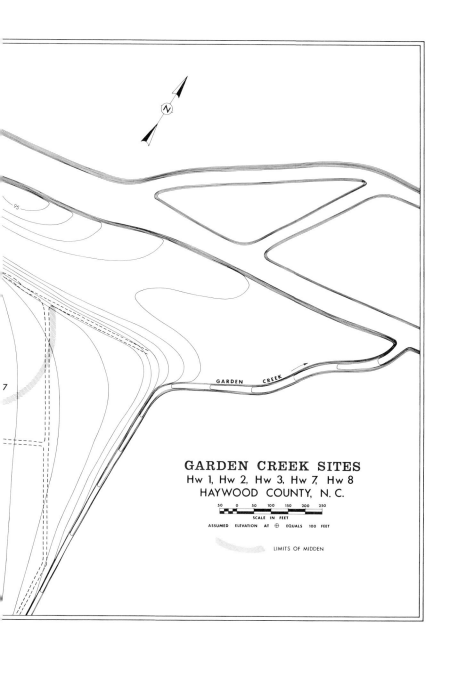

95

7

GARDEN CREEK

GARDEN CREEK SITES
Hw 1, Hw 2, Hw 3, Hw 7, Hw 8
HAYWOOD COUNTY, N. C.

50   0   50   100   150   200   250

SCALE IN FEET

ASSUMED   ELEVATION   AT ⊕ EQUALS   100   FEET

LIMITS OF MIDDEN

"several short, knob-like legs of jars," and "several bottoms of jars of the pointed type" (Heye 1919:38-41). Heye concluded that "the mound was not designed for mortuary purposes," but, instead, that "it was used by the Cherokees in playing their ball game . . . to mark the limits of the ball field" (Heye 1919:38-41).

The earliest investigations of Mound No. 2 were conducted by A. J. Osborne in 1880 for Benjamin B. Valentine of the Valentine Museum, Richmond, Virginia. At that time, it was known as the Smathers' Mound. Osborne dug a hole in the center of the mound and reported to Valentine that:

> Inside the mound was made of loose rich soil, except where the corpses lay, that was made of clay mortar and burned. It was 7 or 8 feet deep. In the center of the mound there were three buried one on top of the other, with about 1½ feet of soil between—and so on all over. These bones were nearly all decayed. I could only tell where they lay by the clay [shell] beads [Osborne n.d.].

In 1965, the highly disturbed remnant of Mound No. 2 measured approximately 110 feet north-south and 150 feet east-west and was 4 feet high. The Research Laboratories' excavations, completed during the 1965 field season, uncovered portions of two early mound stages and an intact house pattern on the premound surface. Ceramic and other remains associated with the early mound stages were predominantly of the Connestee phase. A Connestee pit, intrusive into Mound Stage 1, was dated A.D. 805 ± 85 (GX0593). Artifacts of the Pigeon, Swannanoa, and Savannah River phases were found in the mound fill, but these all were determined to be incidental inclusions and not related to the period of mound construction (Keel 1972:208-212).

Post molds, features, and burial pits of the Pisgah phase occupation (Osborne's burials probably were Pisgah also) intruded into and through the mound stages, but no definite patterns could be discerned. Also, it could not be determined for certain whether the Pisgah people used this mound as a substructure or whether it just happened to be located in the area of their later village activity. When Osborne investigated the mound in 1880, it was estimated by him to be 7 or 8 feet high (see the above quotation). This, together with the stratigraphy of the mound margins (Keel 1972:Figure 3.8), would indicate that there had been additional construction above the two stages revealed by the Research Laboratories' excavations. Either the mound was not used for ceremonial purposes during the

Pisgah period but was simply in the area of the village, it was reused during the Pisgah period in its existing form as a ceremonial substructure, or it was enlarged during the Pisgah period and used as a ceremonial substructure. The latter alternative seems more probable in view of the density of Pisgah features in the mound area proper. This density was roughly equivalent to that of Mound No. 1, a definite Pisgah construction. Keel (1972:111) agrees with this interpretation.

Mound No. 1, the largest of the Garden Creek mounds (Figure 12), was excavated in its entirety by the Research Laboratories during the 1965, 1966, and 1967 seasons. It does not appear that Osborne dug into this mound during his explorations of 1880. His correspondence with Valentine states that permission to dig could not be acquired (Records Relating to the Affairs of the Valentine Brothers, 1879-1880s:46,49). A trench-like disturbance in the center of the mound, penetrating to the bottom, may nevertheless have been the later work of one of the Valentine brothers. A roughly circular disturbance, adjacent to the above-mentioned pit, was dug by local citizens at a more recent date.

In 1919, George G. Heye described Mound No. 1 in the following manner:

> The Richard Plott mound is conical in form and averages eighty feet in diameter by eighteen feet in height. On the sloping side of the mound many potsherds and broken chunkee stones of quartz were found. As before mentioned, in the center of the mound grows an old apple tree. Fifteen feet west of it lay the remains of a burial, consisting of many human bones and a shell bead that had been exposed by plowing. On the same site, but nearer the base of the mound, a deposit of charred acorns and nuts was discovered, and in several places masses of charcoal were seen. This superficial examination was made during a preliminary survey of the valley, when the presence of growing crops made excavation impracticable. During our sojourn the owner of this mound informed us that several human skeletons had been unearthed in plowing its surface [Heye 1919:37].

In 1965, the heavily plowed and eroded mound stood about 7 feet high at the center and measured roughly 130 feet north-south by 150 feet east-west. The initial excavations were in the form of two 5-foot-wide test trenches, one from the northeast and another from the southeast (Plate 20). These were begun well off the mound and were excavated only to the base of the plow zone. Deep cuts into the extant mound were avoided, as they would have mutilated any remaining building surfaces.

PLATE 20. Garden Creek Mound No. 1, with preliminary test trenches, looking west.

When the initial trenches were completed, the remainer of the first season was devoted to clearing the plow zone from the north-east and southeast slopes of the mound and from an area on the eastern periphery (Plate 21). This work revealed sections of two eroded floors, portions of a ramp, and a number of intrusive post molds, pits, and burials. The overall mound conformation was found to be roughly rectangular with the long axis running east-west and the ramp facing east.

Even though the margins of the uppermost floor (Floor 2) had been cut away by erosion, the greater portions of three structural patterns could be detected. These consisted of two superimposed house patterns and a palisaded enclosure. At least seven burials also originated on this floor. Structure A (Figure 13) consisted of an outer wall pattern that measured approximately 28 feet square. The posts were about 0.6 foot in diameter. Three larger inner support post molds measured from 1.6 to 2 feet in diameter. A fourth support post mold at the southeast corner was probably removed by an earlier, unauthorized excavation. Structure B (Figure 13) measured 15 feet square. The outer wall post molds were about 0.6 foot in diameter. In two instances they cut through posts of Structure A. Two sets of entrance wall trenches, one pair extending from the middle of the north wall and another from the northeast corner of the east wall, were associated with this structure. The enclosure (Figure 13) extended around the outer limits of the mound summit. At the corners, particularly at the northwest corner, some post molds in this pattern had been lost to erosion. A gap in the pattern on the east side, in line with the ramp, probably represents an entrance.

On the old village surface, adjacent to the mound, there were numerous post molds and larger basin-shaped pits which presumably were borrow pits for clay used in mound construction. The presence of sherds from the same vessels in several different borrow pits suggests that some of the pits had been opened concurrently. One such pit (Feature 10), located about 30 feet from the southeast toe of the mound, was dated by radiocarbon at A.D. 1435 ± 70 (GX0595).

During the 1966 season, mound outwash zones were removed and the remaining plow zone was stripped from the mound proper and from a narrow perimeter around the base, thereby isolating the entire mound structure. Following this, the east half of the mound (right of the R100 line) was excavated to the level of Floors 1 and 1-A. Plate 22 shows the mound at this stage of excavation, near the

PLATE 21. Garden Creek Mound No. 1, with the plow zone removed from the east half of the mound, looking west.

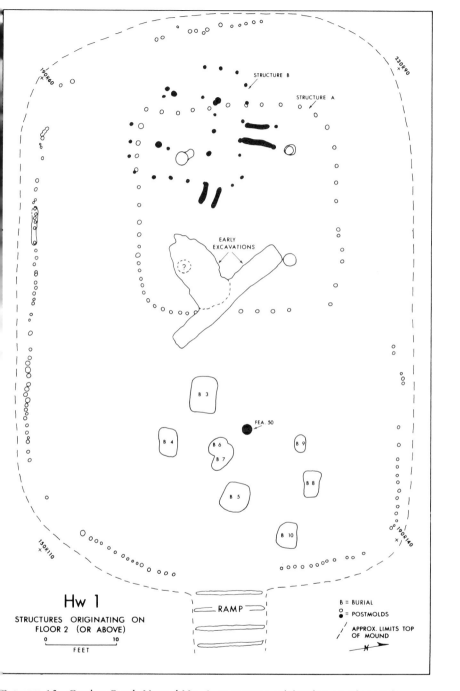

STRUCTURE B

STRUCTURE A

EARLY
EXCAVATIONS

?

B 3

FEA. 50

B 4

B 6

B 7

B 9

B 8

B 5

B 10

Hw 1

STRUCTURES ORIGINATING ON
FLOOR 2 (OR ABOVE)

RAMP

B = BURIAL

○ = POSTMOLDS
●

APPROX. LIMITS TOP
OF MOUND

N

0   10

FEET

FIGURE 13. Garden Creek Mound No. 1, structures originating on Floor 2 (or above).

PLATE 22. Garden Creek Mound No. 1, at the level of Floors 1 and 1-A, looking west.

end of the 1966 season. Clearly visible in this photograph are the two depressed areas which overlay the collapsed premound earth lodges. The fill has been removed from the exposed portion of the depression over Earth Lodge 1 (on the left adjacent to the profile), but the fill has not yet been excavated from the depression over Earth Lodge 2 (rectangular dark area to the right). The only construction feature originating on the surface of Floor 1 was a single wall trench 18 feet long.

The ramp leading to the surface of Floor 1 was defined more clearly in 1966. In addition, the lower two steps of a later and more heavily used ramp were found just to the northeast of the first ramp. The later ramp was wider than the first and probably had led to a surface considerably above either of the extant floors (Plate 22).

The previously mentioned mound outwash, removed during the 1966 season, consisted of two major zones. The outermost of these (Zone B, Figure 14) was composed of erosional deposits that had accumulated after the abandonment of the mound. This was thickest on the northeast and southeast slopes and was relatively barren of artifact remains. The inner zone (Zone A, Figure 14) was composed of refuse and earth that had accumulated around the base of the mound during its last period of use. This deposit, thickest on the northwest or back side of the mound, contained mostly artifacts of the historic period, including glass trade beads, metal objects, Qualla series sherds, ash, and burnt clay. A charcoal sample from Zone A was dated A.D. 1745 ± 65 (GX0729).

Most of the 1967 season was spent in removing the clay cap that formed Floor 1 and the mound fill which underlay Floors 1 and 1-A. The cap was of relatively sterile yellow clay, whereas the fill was composed of dark soil that probably had been obtained near the village. Basket loading was clearly evident throughout these zones.

When the last of the mound fill had been removed, several important premound structural features were revealed. A concentration of river boulders, partly uncovered during the first summer, was found to underlie the entire back (west) two-thirds of the mound. These boulders were uniformly distributed over an area encompassing almost exactly the outer limits of the first mound stage (Plate 23). Many of the boulders were found to be resting on fallen timbers (Plate 24). Also discovered when the rocks were removed was a complex arrangement of post molds, some of which extended as vertical cavities into the overlying mound fill, indicating that some

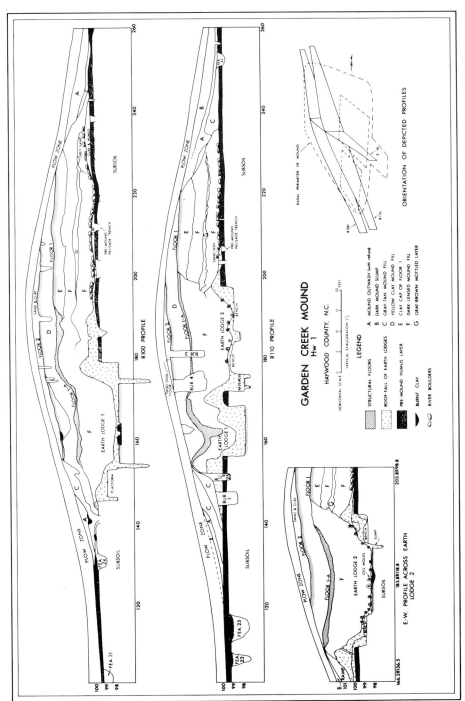

FIGURE 14. Garden Creek Mound No. 1, profiles.

PLATE 23. Concentration of river boulders at the base of Garden Creek Mound No. 1.

PLATE 24. Close-up of boulders and collapsed posts at the base of Garden
Creek Mound No. 1.

of the posts had been standing when the mound was raised to the level of Floor 1. These post molds formed a rectangular pattern measuring about 50 x 70 feet, with eight rows running from east to west within the rectangle. Posts on the outer rows were somewhat larger and more closely spaced than those on the inner rows.

During the removal of the fill from the front (east) one-third of the mound, the excavators encountered two roughly square clay ridges with depressed centers (Plate 25). These were soon found to represent the collapsed remains of semisubterranean earth-covered buildings. The smaller building was designated Earth Lodge 1, and the larger one to the north was designated Earth Lodge 2. The previously described rock mantle and post mold pattern extended onto the flanks of the earth embankments of both buildings, indicating that the buildings had been constructed first.

When the collapsed roof material was removed from the two depressions, the floor plans and associated features of the two buildings were clearly revealed (Plate 26). Earth Lodge 1 had been erected within an excavation which measured roughly 24 feet square and was cut to a depth of 2.2 feet below the existing ground surface. A platform of clay 4.5 x 11 feet across and 1 foot high had been left at the southeast corner. Four central support posts, which measured between 1 and 1.5 feet in diameter, stood approximately 8 feet in from the corners. Outer wall posts were set about 2 feet inside the limits of the excavation. These posts were alternately large and small, the large ones measuring about 0.8 foot in diameter and smaller ones about 0.3 foot. A pair of entrance wall trenches was located on the west side of the structure, and a carefully prepared platform hearth was located at the center of the floor. An interesting feature of the hearth was a narrow, carefully dug drainage trough which surrounded the base of the platform and led to a sump hole on the west side. Remnants of several fallen timbers were found on the earth lodge floor, as were portions of at least three Pisgah vessels. Otherwise, the floor was clean.

Earth Lodge 2 was located immediately to the north of Earth Lodge 1. A connecting passageway provided evidence that the two structures had been used, at least for a time, simultaneously. The supports of this passage were set in wall trenches, in the same manner as the outside entrance of Earth Lodge 1. The excavation for the floor of Earth Lodge 2 was 28 feet square and 1.2 feet deep. An area in the center, roughly 17 feet square, was 0.6 foot deeper. This left a bench about 6 feet wide around the interior of the wall. The

PLATE 25. Garden Creek Mound No. 1, with excavations at mound base, looking west. Boulders are in place, and earth lodge floors are not yet excavated.

PLATE 26. Garden Creek Mound No. 1, at mound base, looking west. Boulders have been partly removed and the earth lodge floors exposed.

height of the bench had been increased another 0.4 foot with the clay excavated from the central area. Impressions of split-cane matting were present in several places on the bench. Four post molds for interior roof supports measured from 1.1 to 1.6 feet in diameter and were placed at points 6 feet in from the walls. The wall posts were set in the bench about 1 foot inside the margins of the excavation. These posts were uniformly about 0.8 foot in diameter. The central hearth consisted of a roughly oval basin that measured 4 x 6 feet across and was about 0.4 foot deep in the center. A narrow trough originated just to the northeast of the hearth and led to a sump next to the west bench. Numerous horizontal molds of fallen roof beams and cane roof covering were present on the floor and benches. Associated artifacts consisted of a few animal bones and portions of a Pisgah Check Stamped vessel.

The collapsed roof material in both earth lodges formed a rather thin (about 0.4 to 0.6 foot) layer over the central portion of the floor, suggesting that there had been only a sparse covering of dirt on the upper portions of the roofs. This layer was much thicker (about 1 to 3 feet) around the walls and the roof margins. The profile cuts made across the intersection of the roof fill of the two lodges revealed that Earth Lodge 1 had been erected before Earth Lodge 2.

Following excavation of the earth lodges and removal of the rock mantle, it was found that these ceremonial structures had been erected over an earlier portion of the Pisgah village. A significant feature at this premound level was a palisade, approximately 100 feet of which was revealed in the area of excavation. This palisade was oriented east-west and was set in a trench similar to Palisade D at the Warren Wilson site. It had a 10 x 15 foot rectangular offset on the south side at the location later occupied by Earth Lodge 2. This offset obviously represents a bastion. Part of another probable offset was recorded in the extreme western limit of excavation, about 65 feet west of the first one. Bastions were not found on the palisades at the Warren Wilson site.

Twenty-four burials were encountered in the excavation of Mound No. 1. These originated on Floor 2, in the flanks of the mound at the stage of Floor 2 or later, and in the premound humus. Others were intrusive through Floor 2, having originated from higher levels.[7]

7. See Ch. 3 for additional information on these burials.

A hypothetical reconstruction of the sequence of ceremonial constructions at Mound No. 1 begins with the erection of a semisubterranean, earth-covered building on a portion of the old village surface. After a relatively brief period of time, a second earth lodge was built adjacent to the original structure, and the two were then used simultaneously. Following the completion of the earth lodges, and again after some unknown interval of time, a multicorridored arrangement of posts was set up adjacent to the lodges. It is not known whether this elaborate construction was roofed. It is possible that there was some form of lightweight covering, consisting of straw or small branches, which would have created a large open-air structure such as might have been used for public gatherings during the warmer months.

Either at a point when the earth lodges were becoming dilapidated or at a time when some social or religious event signaled the need for new ceremonial architecture, a layer of boulders was placed over the area of the post construction and onto the west flanks of the earth lodges. Some posts were left standing, but rocks were laid directly on top of those that had fallen. Then, basketloads of soil collected from old midden areas were piled over the rocks and remaining posts. This fill was raised nearly to the height of the earth lodge roofs, and then a cap of clean yellow clay was spread over the top of the fill and up to but not covering the tops of the earth lodges. On this surface (Floor 1) a construction was begun, but it was only partly finished when the earth lodge roofs collapsed, creating two large concavities on the front floor of the mound. When these depressions had been filled with more midden soil, the old roof areas were covered with a thin cap of clay (Floor 1-A). This provided a clay floor over the entire raised surface, which at this time measured approximately 50 x 70 feet.

Before this surface could be put to use, however, the earth lodges collapsed further, resulting in the addition of a completely new cap of clay over the entire mound. This surface (Floor 2) was covered with a thin layer of clean sand. Although Floor 2 continued to sag on the east side, it was stable enough to serve as the base for the first completed ceremonial constructions. At least two buildings were erected at different periods on the more trustworthy western portion of Floor 2, a total of seven burials was placed in the eastern portion, and a log palisade was built around the entire top perimeter. The mound went through several building stages subsequent to Floor 2, and its final use was during the Qualla period.

VILLAGE AREA

Excavations by the Research Laboratories at the Garden Creek site were restricted primarily to the two remaining mounds. The village midden around Mound No. 2 (designated Hw 8) was not explored. However, the village midden adjacent to Mound No. 1 (designated Hw 7) was tested to some extent in the area immediately east of the mound. Here, a 100 x 100 foot section of plow zone was stripped and the features were recorded and excavated. An additional area of 30 x 35 feet was opened a short distance to the east of the above excavations after plowing had turned up charred wood and burnt clay.

Two probable house patterns were located in the area immediately east of the mound, and a definite house floor was found beneath the area of plowed-up refuse. The two house patterns nearest the mound, although not clearly defined, appeared as clusters of post molds roughly 20 feet square. Each cluster was accompanied by a pair of entrance trenches. In one instance the entrance was at the southwest corner, facing south; in the other it was at the northwest corner, facing north.

The house floor detected through plow disturbance consisted of a well-defined, shallow depression that measured 18 x 20 feet (Plate 27). The long axis was northwest to southeast. Charred timbers, fragments of charred cane matting (Plate 28), and patches of ash, mussel shells, and animal bones were scattered over the floor. Also on the floor were three burials, several refuse filled pits, and a central fire basin that measured 4.8 feet in diameter. A post mold pattern was well defined only along the southeast side of the floor. The post molds were from 0.6 to 0.8 foot in diameter and were set at intervals of about 2 feet, and most of them contained the remnants of charred posts, further evidence that this structure had burned.

OTHER MOUND SITES HAVING POSSIBLE PISGAH AFFILIATIONS

Pisgah ceramics have been found, either in surface collections or through test excavations, at a number of mound sites in western North Carolina. In no case, however—except at the Garden Creek site—can any particular phase in the construction of these mounds be attributed positively to the Pisgah phase. These sites (Figures 1

PLATE 27. House floor in the village area (Hw 7) at the Garden Creek site.

PLATE 28. Charred split-cane matting on the house floor in the village area (Hw 7) at the Garden Creek site.

and 2) include the Nuquasee Mound and Cowee Mound on the Little Tennessee River in Macon County; the Sawnooke Mound (probably on the location of the historic town of Nununyi) and the Birdtown Mound on the Oconaluftee River in Swain County; the Rogers' Mound located near the juncture of Cullowee Creek and the Tuckasegee River in Jackson County; the Kituhwa or Governor's Island Mound on the Tuckasegee River in Swain County; and the Wells' Mound (specific location unknown) on the Pigeon River a short distance from the Garden Creek site (information obtained from the files of the Research Laboratories of Anthropology, Chapel Hill, North Carolina, and the Valentine Museum, Richmond, Virginia).

The number of Pisgah sherds in the collections from most of these sites was small, usually amounting to less than 5 percent. At the Sawnooke Mound, however, Pisgah sherds numbered 34 out of a total of 218 surviving from excavations made by Edward P. Valentine in 1882. Valentine's work at this mound was surprisingly good for its day. He took special note of a layer of river boulders at the bottom of the mound:

> The rocks were very large rolled stones from the river. This pile of stones reached from 3 ft. below the surface to the bottom of the mound and had there a base of 21½ ft. diam.—they however were not supported but were pushed into this position with the earth of Mound. The laying of them was rough [Valentine n.d.:9-10].

This feature, along with the Pisgah sherds, makes it probable that at least a portion of the Sawnooke Mound was constructed during the Pisgah phase.

Cyrus Thomas (1894:350) reported finding a mound in Buncombe County, near Asheville. The site has not been relocated, but since there is little or no evidence for historic occupations in the Swannanoa Valley, it is possible that this was a Pisgah mound. Thomas' description reads:

> This mound is about 4 miles from Asheville on the bottom land, not more than 100 yards from the river, is circular, 80 feet in diameter, and 9 feet high. A wide trench cut through it from side to side and down to the natural soil brought to light the fact that it was built partly of stone and partly of earth. The core or central portion, to the height of 4 feet above the original surface and covering a space about 30 feet in diameter, was built of irregular blocks of stone, heaped together without order or plan. The remainder of the mound was made of dark surface soil. The top layer of earth being removed down to the rock pile, the entire surface of the latter was

found to be covered with charcoal and evidences that it had been burned here. Among the coal were numerous joints of charred cane [Thomas 1894: 350].

The "rock pile," possibly a mantle as at Garden Creek Mound No. 1, lends support to the idea that this was a Pisgah mound.

The Lindsey Mound, on the west bank of the North Saluda River in Greenville County, South Carolina, is another small platform mound having possible Pisgah affiliations. A shaft was dug into the top of this mound in 1917, and the excavator reported finding two burials and a series of superimposed floors with baked-clay hearths (Bragg 1918:19-20). The report describes no artifacts, other than ashes and animal bone, but Pisgah sherds have been found in a cultivated field to the south and east of the mound and in a small area of eroding midden immediately to the northwest (Wesley Breedlove, personal communication).

Pisgah sherds have been found at the Loy site on the east bank of the Holston River in Jefferson County, Tennessee, where a palisade and ditch surround a substructure mound and a 6-acre occupation area. The mound is thought to be the product of a Dallas occupation, and not of an earlier and sparsely represented Pisgah occupation (Richard Polhemus, personal communication).

In 1881, Edward Palmer investigated a mound at the confluence of the Pigeon and French Broad rivers in Cocke County, Tennessee (Holmes 1884:440). Descriptions of the pottery found in this mound (see Chapter 5) provide evidence for an association with the Pisgah phase. William H. Holmes reported:

> The mound from which these [pottery] fragments were obtained was located 3 miles from Newport. It was 12 [120?] feet square and 6 feet high. The original height was probably much greater. The pottery was mixed with ashes and debris of what appeared to be three fire-places. No human remains were found [Holmes 1884:440].

Mounds excavated by the Smithsonian Institution in the Norris Basin on the lower Clinch and Powell rivers are also important. Although substantial amounts of Pisgah pottery have been recently reported for sites in this same general area (Richard Polhemus, personal communication), no such ceramics were described or illustrated in the Norris Basin report (Webb 1938). However, structural features of several of the mounds were comparable to those at Garden Creek Mound No. 1. At the base of the platform mound at the Lee Farm site, there was a floor "with an oval ridge about the edge"

(Webb 1938:146 and Plate 96a), possibly the marginal remnant of an earthen roof covering (compare with profiles of Garden Creek Mound No. 1, Figure 14). At the Cox Mound there was another possible earth-covered structure, over the remains of which were "more than 200 irregular rocks" (Webb 1938:163, 167 and Plates 128-131).

Two mound sites on the lower French Broad River, Fain's Island and Zimmerman's Island, contained small amounts of Pisgah pottery. Both sites, excavated by the University of Tennessee in the late 1930s, are now inundated by Douglas Reservoir. Although a minor Pisgah component was found at each of these sites, the major occupations and ones responsible for the platform mounds appear to have been in the protohistoric and historic periods (Richard Polhemus, personal communication).

PISGAH HOUSES AT THE McCULLOUGH BEND AND COBB ISLAND SITES, TENNESSEE

Richard Polhemus has conducted test excavations at two Pisgah sites in northeastern Tennessee. At the McCullough Bend site, located on an island in the Clinch River, he uncovered two house floors with associated Pisgah ceramics. Since this site is partially covered by Norris Lake, work had to be conducted when the water level was low. Polhemus (personal communication) summarized the architectural data as follows:

> One structure was totally excavated; one was outlined but not excavated to the floor level. They were rectangular house structures with the floor level at least one foot below present ground surface. They each had an entrance on the northwest side. Post molds (shallow and of small diameter) ringed the perimeter of the house floor. Posts at the corners and on each side of the entrance were larger and deeper than the wall posts. There was a hearth in the center represented by a fired area on the floor. There was a clay seat or bench against the northeast wall. Interior postmolds were present.

Other features of Pisgah provenience at this site were pits and hearths containing quantities of fire-broken rock, Pisgah sherds, and bone (Richard Polhemus, personal communication).

At the Cobb Island Site on the Holston River, Polhemus excavated another house floor of probable Pisgah provenience.

Test excavations near the center of Cobb Island, on a slight rise, produced evidence of a substantial burned structure having a floor situated 20
to 21 inches below the present ground surface. The structure was set in a pit
nearly 18 inches in depth, which resulted in a standing fired daub wall of
this height in the southwest corner. A large quantity of charred structural
material, composed of grass, bark, cane, and posts was present on the floor,
under and mixed with the daub from the walls. A number of Pisgah sherds
and a triangular projectile point were recovered from a floor context. The
structure was rectangular with enclosed corners and relatively large wall
posts [Richard Polhemus, personal communication].

A single burial, accompanied by two Dallas Cord Marked vessels,
was found near the above structure. The burial fill contained nine
Pisgah Complicated Stamped sherds.

PISGAH SETTLEMENT PATTERNS

Data obtained thus far support the following interpretation of
Pisgah settlement patterns, at least during the late subphase (ca. A.D.
1250-1450). It must be emphasized, however, that considerably
more information is needed than that provided by partial excavation of two sites and incomplete survey coverage.

Pisgah villages ranged in size from only a few houses to perhaps
as many as 50 houses and were distributed in varying densities along
major streams and in the tributary valleys, on or adjacent to fertile
bottomland soils. Presumably, portions of the bottomlands adjacent
to each village were maintained as agricultural plots. A typical village (Figure 15) contained houses that were constructed on a square
or slightly rectangular plan with rounded corners. The walls of these
houses were formed of closely spaced upright posts and covered
with bark or woven-cane mats. The roofs were peaked at the center
where there was a smoke hole, and probably were covered with
bark shingles or straw thatch. The floor of a house was slightly
lower than the surrounding ground, and there was a raised clay
hearth at the center. The interior of a house might be divided into
several small rooms, and the entrance was usually a vestibule that
extended a short distance out from one of the walls. Storage pits,
refilled borrow pits, and refilled burials were located on the house
floor or just outside of the house.

In a village, houses were arranged in a roughly circular or oval
pattern facing a central plaza. Adjacent to some of the houses were

FIGURE 15. Artist's conception of the Pisgah village at the Warren Wilson site at an early stage in the development of the village.

smaller structures, possibly used for sweat baths, winter sleeping quarters, or storage bins. Probably, there were also skinning racks, fences, small garden plots, and additional hearths or pottery kilns interspersed between the houses. The village was surrounded by a sturdy log palisade which had an overlap on one side for an entrance. At some villages, perhaps the larger and more important ones, the palisades were equipped with bastions. These palisades, probably for defensive purposes, were enlarged as the villages grew.

Certain large villages contained ceremonial facilities, which might consist of (singly or in combination) semisubterranean earth lodges, large open-air structures, or houses raised on earthen platforms. Such buildings probably were reserved for political and religious functions, and possibly also served as residences of priests or ranking members of the community. It is likely that groups of villages were allied to these larger "ceremonial centers," but the boundaries of these groupings and the nature of the allegiances are yet to be defined.

AREAL RELATIONSHIPS

Houses with the same general architectural features as Pisgah houses have been found on late prehistoric sites over much of the eastern United States. However, two features seem to have rather restricted distribution. The distinctive vestibule entrance is found on houses of the Mouse Creek phase in southeastern Tennessee (Lewis and Kneberg 1941:7-8), the Barnett phase (late Dallas and Lamar) in northwestern Georgia (Garrow and Smith 1973:11-19), the Pee Dee phase on the North and South Carolina Piedmont (Joffre Coe, personal communication), and the Savannah and Irene phases on the Georgia-South Carolina Coastal Plain (Caldwell and McCann 1941:35-36, 74). Subfloor burials are associated with the Wilbanks phase of north-central Georgia (Larson 1971:66) and the Barnett phase of northwestern Georgia (Garrow and Smith 1973: 5-10).

A comparable settlement plan,[8] in which houses are arranged in a circular pattern around a plaza and within a palisade, has been recorded at the Mouse Creek site on the Hiwassee River in southeastern Tennessee (Kneberg 1952:198 and Figure 110), the King site or

8. Complete or even partial settlement plans have been obtained from only a few sites in the Southeast.

the Coosa River in northwestern Georgia (Garrow n.d.:2-4), the Town Creek site on the Little River in south-central North Carolina (Joffre Coe, personal communication), and the Slone site on the Levisa Fork of the Big Sandy River in southeastern Kentucky (Dunnell, Hanson, and Hardesty 1971:4-6). At the Mouse Creek and King sites, a shallow ditch, adjacent to the outside of the palisade, surrounded the village. A ditch was not found at either Warren Wilson or Garden Creek, but excavations were not carried to the outermost limits of either site.

The overall community plan at the Slone site was very similar to that suggested by the excavations at the Warren Wilson site. At Slone, a roughly circular palisade, with an overlapping entrance, surrounded the village. This enclosure was enlarged at least twice, with the final stage incorporating about 2 acres. Houses were square or rectangular with rounded corners, a central fire basin, and interior roof supports. Storage pits, garbage pits, fire pits, and graves were found on the house floors and between the houses and the palisade. The houses faced a central plaza that was devoid of features and cultural refuse. The largest concentrations of refuse, especially food remains and potsherds, were found along the inside margins of the palisades (Dunnell, Hanson, and Hardesty 1971:7-43 and Figures 18, 28).

Traits represented in Pisgah mound construction and ceremonial architecture at the Garden Creek site have been found at other sites in the Southern Appalachians. The Peachtree Mound, on the Hiwassee River in southwestern North Carolina, had comparable construction phases to Garden Creek Mound No. 1. These were summarized by Setzler and Jennings (1941:28):

> Upon this village site was built a hard-packed area which later became the floor of a large ceremonial structure of stone and wood. This was covered by a small round-topped mound, about 60 feet in diameter. Over this mound, and separated from it by a sand stratum, was a larger secondary mound which underwent at least two major periods of construction and several minor additions. The secondary mound had upon it three successive ceremonial buildings, as evidenced by the three superimposed floors.

The stone portion of the initial submound structure at Peachtree was thought by the excavators to represent a "bench" (Setzler and Jennings 1941:24). However, the photographs taken of this feature shortly after its discovery show that it almost certainly was a stone mantle similar to the one at Garden Creek Mound No. 1 (Setzler

and Jennings 1941:Plates 4A, 4C, 5B, 6B). And a close look at the
illustrations of the mound profiles (Plates 2, 3) reveals that there
was a depressed area in the central part of the mound, possibly the
remains of a collapsed earth-covered structure.[9] Although a few Pisgah sherds were recovered at Peachtree (Setzler and Jennings 1941:
Plates 37, 43), the mound seems to have been primarily constructed
in the Dallas and Qualla phases.

At the Nacoochee Mound, located on the upper Chattahoochee
River in northeastern Georgia, a stone layer was present on the premound surface. This layer of "rough pieces" and "boulders" measured 25.5 feet across and averaged 2 feet in depth, and many of the
stones rested on "pieces of bark" (Heye, Hodge, and Pepper 1918:
34). A few Pisgah-like sherds were found at Nacoochee, but the majority of the ceramics belong to the Wilbanks, Dallas, and Lamar (or
Qualla) phases.

At the Chauga site, located at the confluence of the Tugaloo and
Chauga rivers in northwestern South Carolina, certain mound features were similar to Garden Creek Mound No. 1 (Kelly and Neitzel
1961:10-20). There were thin clay-and-sand caps over successive
mound stages, collections of boulders incorporated into mound
construction, a palisaded enclosure associated with mound margins,
and clay "embankments" around early mound structures (possibly
the remnants of earth lodges). The Chauga Mound contained artifacts from the Etowah, Wilbanks, and Lamar (or Qualla) phases.

The remains of a group of earth-covered buildings have been discovered at the base of the Bell Field Mound at Carter's Quarters on
the Coosawatee River in northwest Georgia, in association with the
Wilbanks phase at that site. These were square buildings with depressed floors, low benches around the interior walls, and central
fire basins. There was evidence to suggest that two of the structures
were conjoined, similar to Earth Lodges 1 and 2 at the Garden
Creek site (A. R. Kelly, personal communication).

The Wilbanks Mound on the Etowah River in north-central Georgia contained at its core an earth-covered structure quite similar to
the ones excavated at Garden Creek Mound No. 1 (Sears 1958:129-
194). The structure did not have a subsurface floor as at Garden
Creek, but apart from this it appears to have been constructed in
much the same manner. Sears' interpretation (1958:142-144 and
Figure 5) of the roof as having slanted rafters "held in the proper

9. Sears (1958:417) has also proposed that the initial structure at the Peachtree Mound
was an earth lodge.

angled position across the top of the large horizontal logs used to outline the structure" seems untenable to me (it is difficult to believe that such a roof could have supported the weight of even a thin layer of earth). Sears might have found vertical wall posts had he removed all of the collapsed soil from the wall buttress. The Wilbanks Mound dates to the late Etowah and early Wilbanks phases of the Etowah drainage (Sears 1958:171). The possible remains of sub-mound earth lodges were found at two other Etowah Valley sites—the Long Swamp and Horseshoe Bend sites—by Wauchope (1966: 303, 324). These mounds also are attributed to the late Etowah and Wilbanks phases.

The remains of an earth-covered structure were encountered at the base of the Pee Dee phase mound at the Town Creek site on the Little River in south-central North Carolina. Construction features of this building were similar to those at Garden Creek Mound No. 1, with the only difference being that the floor of the Town Creek structure was not subterranean. All of the mound structures at Town Creek also had exterior vestibule entrances (Joffre Coe, personal communication).

Circular earth-covered ceremonial buildings were found at the Ocmulgee and Brown's Mount sites on the Ocmulgee River in Bibb County, Georgia (Fairbanks 1946:94-108). These were large (28 to 42 feet in diameter) buildings, with long passageway entrances, clay benches around the walls, large interior roof supports, and central fire basins. At the Ocmulgee site, the largest and best preserved of these structures (usually referred to as the Macon Earth Lodge) had an elaborate eagle-effigy platform opposite the entrance, and around the remaining wall there was a clay bench with 47 equally spaced rectangular seats. This structure has been radiocarbon dated at A.D. 1015 ± 110 (I-981) and is associated with the Macon Plateau phase of central Georgia (Wilson 1964:202-203).

TEMPORAL RELATIONSHIPS

There is some evidence to support the existence of wall-post houses and earthen platform mounds in the Appalachian Summit prior to the Pisgah phase. A relatively pure component of the Connestee phase at the Gashes Creek site contained an abundance of post molds, but unfortunately only limited excavations were conducted and no complete structural patterns were defined. However, a square post mold pattern was found at Garden Creek Mound No. 2 on the earliest mound stage which was constructed late in the Connestee phase, around A.D. 800.

A continuation of Pisgah-type house architecture, mound construction, and settlement pattern into the Qualla phase, and therefore into the historic Cherokee setting, has been amply documented at the Coweeta Creek site on the Little Tennessee River in southwestern North Carolina. This site consisted of a group of houses, having identical construction features to the Pisgah houses, arranged around a plaza. There was a low mound surmounted by a ceremonial structure at one end of the plaza and possibly another ceremonial structure at the opposite end. Excavations were not carried far enough to determine whether the village was palisaded (Egloff 1971:42 and Figure 4). A suggested dating would place the Qualla occupation at Coweeta Creek in the 17th and early 18th centuries (Joffre Coe, personal communication). A rock mantle, quite similar to the one found at the base of Garden Creek Mound No. 1, was present in a historic Cherokee mound at the Estatoe site in northeastern Georgia (de Baillou and Kelly 1960:1-30), and possibly at the Coweeta Creek Mound (Egloff 1971:53).

Perhaps the most obvious change in mound architecture from the Pisgah phase to the historic Cherokee period was an abandonment of the use of massive construction stages. For example, Garden Creek Mound No. 1 was composed of a sequence of thick fill layers and clay caps, whereas the Coweeta Creek Mound represented little more than the accumulation of one thin floor over another.

Earth-covered ceremonial buildings, similar to the ones found beneath Garden Creek Mound No. 1, definitely were used by the Cherokees until the late historic period. William Bartram, on his visit to the Middle Town of Cowe in 1776, described a "large rotunda capable of accommodating several hundred people: it stands at the top of an ancient artificial mount of earth . . . . [and has] a thin superficies of earth over all" (Bartram 1791:297-298). Henry Timberlake described the "townhouse" at Chote in the Overhill towns as being "raised with wood, and covered over with earth, and has all the appearance of a small mountain at a little distance" (Timberlake 1765:59).

During the Pisgah phase, the people of the Appalachian Summit region developed a pattern of settlement which had counterparts in neighboring Mississippian cultures. Villages were positioned on river bottomland, their individual layouts were ordered and compact, and considerable attention was paid to the construction and maintenace of ceremonial and civic facilities at certain sites. The people lavished great care on the construction of semisubterranean earth lodges and in the sequential raising of platform mounds. This pattern, begun perhaps as early as A.D. 1000, persisted into the historic period, where it can be identified with Cherokee Indian culture.

3. Burials

Practices that surround the burial of the dead represent some of the most conservative and traditional aspects of cultural behavior. It is fortunate, therefore, that the limited excavations thus far conducted on Pisgah sites have produced a reasonably good sample of burial data.

Thirty-five burials were uncovered in the three seasons at the Warren Wilson site, twenty-seven at Garden Creek Mound No. 1, and eight at Garden Creek Mound No. 2. There is a small amount of additional information from sites in Tennessee and South Carolina. Each burial from the Warren Wilson site is described in detail, and general observations (taken from field reports) are provided on the burials from the Garden Creek site.

Patterns of burial traits are noted, and an effort is made to determine the distribution of these traits in the Southern Appalachians on a comparable time level to Pisgah. Finally, relationships between Pisgah burial traits and those of the Qualla phase are considered. Physical anthropological analyses of the skeletal remains have not yet been conducted, and observations are limited to determining sex and age.[1]

WARREN WILSON SITE

It became obvious early in the work at the Warren Wilson site that burial pits were clustered in and around the houses. These pits appeared as distinct discolorations at the base of the plow zone. Usually subsoil clay was mixed in the pit fill, giving it a mottled appearance, which differed from the typically homogeneous dark fill of other pits.

---

1. I determined age on the basis of tooth eruption and wear, endocranial suture closure, pubic symphysial development, and epiphyseal union. Sexing was based on overall bone robusticity and on size and shape of the mandibular symphysis, mastoid process, sciatic notch, iliac crest, and acetabulum.

Three distinct varieties of burial pit were encountered. The first (Figure 16, left) was a simple pit, which usually was oblong in plan and had rather straight sides and a flat bottom. The second (Figure 16, middle) was a central-chamber variety, in which the initial pit had a smaller excavation in the bottom to contain the corpse, and the resulting shelf was used to support a log covering. In a third variety (Figure 16, right), the initial pit was either oblong or circular and had a chamber recessed in the base of one of the walls. The floor of the chamber was slightly deeper than the floor of the shaft, and there was usually evidence for a slanted covering, either of logs or in one case of flat stones. This latter variety was referred to as a side-chamber burial.

Before beginning excavation of a burial pit, the surface on which it appeared was carefully troweled to ascertain the extent of the pit walls, and photographs were taken for future reference. Next, the area surrounding the pit was covered with boards to shield the surface (which might contain other unexcavated pits and post molds) and to protect the edges of the burial pit itself during excavation. The pit fill was either fine-screened on the site, or, if there were indications that it contained abundant refuse, was stored in boxes for processing at the laboratory. As the removal of the pit fill progressed, the excavator would leave a thin buffer of fill around the walls of the pit. When the level of the bones was reached, this buffer was carefully removed to expose the original pit walls. In this way, there was little destruction to the walls, and it was often possible to detect aboriginal digging marks.

Because of a highly acid and moisture-holding subsoil clay, skeletal remains frequently were in a poor state of preservation and the bones had to be cleaned in place and treated with a water-soluble acrylic (Bedacryl 277) before they were allowed to dry. Prior to the removal of the bones, scale drawings were made, photographs were taken in color and black and white, and all other pertinent information was recorded. As little cleaning as possible was given the pelvic bones and skull. These complex bones usually were removed on pedestals of clay, placed in wooden boxes, and taken to the laboratory for final cleaning, preservation, and reconstruction.

The following are descriptions of each burial, giving the location, type of pit, position and orientation of the skeleton, and a list of associated artifacts.

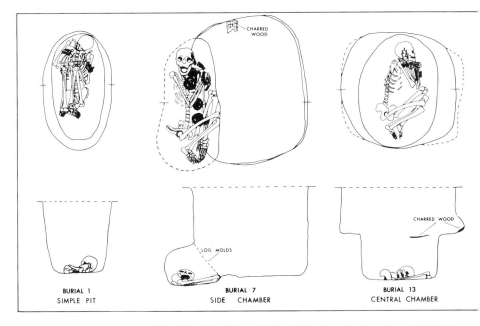

CHARRED
WOOD

LOG MOLDS

CHARRED WOOD

BURIAL 1
SIMPLE PIT

BURIAL 7
SIDE CHAMBER

BURIAL 13
CENTRAL CHAMBER

FIGURE 16. Burial 1 (simple pit), Burial 7 (side chamber), and Burial 13 (central chamber) at the Warren Wilson site.

Burial 1:

Burial 1 (Plate 29) was located at the approximate center of House A (Figure 6), but it could not be assigned to either specific phase of the structure (A^1 or A^2). Patches of burnt clay partially covered the pit, suggesting that this burial, as with several others on the site, was purposely placed in a central position in the house (Figure 6). It was a simple pit with vertical walls and a flat bottom. The orifice was oblong, 2.5 feet wide x 4 feet long, and the depth of the pit from the bottom of the plowed soil was 2.6 feet. The skeleton was in a good state of preservation and was determined to be a female, age 30 to 35 years. The body had been placed on its back with the legs pulled up in a tightly flexed position, the arms crossed over the chest, and the head pointed to the southeast. There were no artifacts accompanying this burial.

Burial 2:

This burial was located a few feet northwest of Burial 1. It, too, was associated with House A, but no assignment to a specific construction phase could be made. The pit, clearly intrusive through Palisade D, measured 3.3 feet long, 2.6 feet wide, and 2.6 feet deep. The sides were vertical, and the floor was flat. The poorly preserved skeletal remains were of a 40- to 50-year-old male. The body had been placed on its left side with the head to the northwest, the legs flexed, and the hands at the knees. There were no grave goods.

Burial 3:

This burial was on the floor of House B^2. The pit was almost circular. It measured 2.6 x 2.8 feet across the top and was 2.2 feet deep. All that remained of the interment was a small organic stain and the tooth crowns. These were determined to have belonged to an infant or newborn, sex undetermined. No grave goods were present.

Burial 4:

This burial was in the southwest corner of the floor of House A^2. It was intrusive through the line of post molds on the outer wall of House A^1. The simple pit measured 3.2 x 2.2 feet across the top and 1.8 feet deep. The skeleton was almost completely decomposed with only the teeth and a few fragments of long bone remaining. It was estimated that the remains were of a child, 3 to 6 years old, sex undetermined. The body was tightly flexed on its left side, with the head to the west. No artifacts accompanied the burial.

Burial 5:

Burial 5 was located a few feet northeast of Burial 3 and also was on the floor of House B^2. The simple pit was 1.5 x 2.7 feet across and 1.8 feet deep. A small cluster of bones and teeth, found at the approximate center of the pit floor, was determined to have belonged to an infant, 6

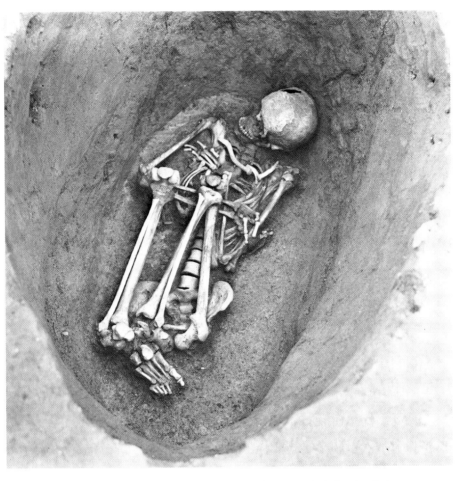

PLATE 29. Burial 1 at the Warren Wilson site, a typical simple-pit interment.

months to 2 years of age, sex undetermined. Grouped with the bones were four shell gorgets (Plate 63) and eight perforated *Marginella* shells.

Burial 6:

Burial 6, also on the floor of House B^2, was located a few feet to the southeast of Burial 5. The pit was of the side-chamber variety. The orifice of the shaft measured 2.1 x 2.5 feet and 1.8 feet deep. The chamber, offset in the bottom of the north wall, measured 2.7 feet long, 1.5 feet wide, and 1.1 feet from ceiling to floor. The floor of the chamber was 0.6 foot below the floor of the shaft. A row of short logs, covered by a layer of bark, had protected the opening of the chamber. The charred ends of two of the logs and a lens of decayed bark were still present. The skeletal remains were located in the east end of the chamber. They were surrounded by a layer of organic material, possibly the remains of a garment or skin wrapping. The bones were of an infant, less than 6 months in age, sex undetermined. Accompanying the burial were 31 small tubular shell beads.

Burial 7:

This burial (Figure 16; Plates 30, 31) was located at the center of the floor of House B^2. The upper portion of the pit fill contained several chunks of burnt clay, probably from the central hearth of the house. Additional concentrations of this clay were found in the plowed soil overlying the burial pit. The pit, nearly rectangular in shape, was 4 feet wide, 5 feet long, and 3 feet deep. The chamber was recessed in the bottom of the south wall of the pit and contained loose, dark fill (Plate 30). The chamber measured 4.4 feet long, 2 feet wide, and 1.3 feet from ceiling to floor. The floor was 0.4 foot below the floor of the shaft. A single section of charred log was all that remained of the covering over the chamber. The well-preserved skeletal remains were of a robust male, 35 to 40 years old at death. The body had been placed in the chamber on its back with the legs flexed to the left side and the head to the northwest. The right arm lay across the chest, and the left arm was extended beside the body and under the legs.

A piece of cut mica was found directly above the skull. One bone awl lay against the left side of the skull, and another was in front of the mandible. A small uncut conch shell filled with red ocher rested on the left shoulder. Additional red ocher, mixed with garfish (*Lepisosteus* sp.) scales, was scattered around the shell. Just above the left shoulder, there was a cluster of six bones, identified as the terminal phalanges of a large panther *(Felis concolor)*. In the neck area, there were 18 small cut mica discs (32 to 42 mm in diameter), and distributed along the front of the skeleton, beginning in the upper chest area and ending in the abdominal area, were 4 large cut mica discs (each about 82 mm in diameter). Two columella bead bracelets, eight beads each, were located at the wrists. The artifacts from Burial 7 are illustrated in Plates 44, 52, 54, and 55.

PLATE 30. Burial 7 at the Warren Wilson site, a typical side-chamber interment before excavation of the chamber.

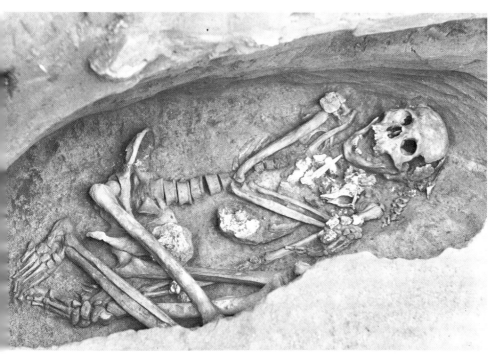

PLATE 31. Burial 7 at the Warren Wilson site, completely excavated.

Burial 8:

This was a simple-pit interment located a few feet to the south of Burial 7 on the floor of House B^2. The pit measured 2.2 x 4 feet across the top and was 2.6 feet deep. It was intersected on the south side by Feature 53. The remains were of a 25- to 30-year-old female. The body had been placed in the pit on its back with the legs flexed to the left side, the arms crossed over the body just below the chest, and the head to the west. The bones were in a poor state of preservation, and there were no grave goods.

Burial 9:

This was a side-chamber interment located at the southeast corner of the floor of House C. Due to the depth of plowing and erosion in this area, the chamber had been truncated, and the pit appeared as a double-lobed intrusion at the base of the plowed soil. The shaft measured 2 x 2.2 feet across the top and 0.5 foot deep. The chamber, on the south side of the shaft, measured 2.4 x 1.6 feet and was 0.4 foot deeper than the shaft. The skeletal remains were found in a small cluster at the west end of the chamber. They were of an infant or newborn, sex undetermined. Included with the burial were 20 columella beads, a shell gorget (Lick Creek style), and 27 small tubular shell beads. The columella beads, grouped in two separate piles of 10 beads each, may represent bracelets.

Burial 10:

Burial 10 was located immediately south of House C and possibly was associated with that structure. The oval-shaped simple pit measured 3.3 feet long and 4.2 feet wide. Erosion had reduced the overlying soil so that the bottom of the pit was only 0.9 foot below the plow line. The skeletal remains, in a fair state of preservation, were of a 23- to 28-year-old male. The body had been placed in the pit on its left side in a tightly flexed position with the head to the west. There were no accompanying artifacts.

Burial 11:

Burial 11 was a side-chamber interment located just outside of the northeast corner of House C. Two post molds of the house were intrusive through the west edge of the burial pit. The shaft measured 2.4 x 4.2 feet across the top and 1.1 feet deep (severe erosion in this area). The chamber was on the south side of the shaft and measured 2.6 x 3.7 feet; it was 0.5 foot deeper than the floor of the shaft. The skeletal remains were in a very poor state of preservation, leaving only one long bone fragment, a few skull fragments, and the teeth. These remains were of a child, age 5 to 10 years, sex undetermined. The body probably had been placed on its back with the legs drawn up to the left side and the head oriented in a westward direction.

Burial 12:

Burial 12, in a central-chamber pit, was located on the east portion of the floor of House E^2. The shaft was approximately circular with a diameter of 2.3 feet and a depth (to the top of the ledge) of 1.2 feet. The chamber measured 1.5 feet wide, 2 feet long, and 0.5 feet deep. The skeletal remains were clustered in the northwest end of the chamber. They were of an infant or newborn, sex undetermined. There were six small tubular shell beads included with the burial.

Burial 13:

This burial (Figure 16; Plate 32), located to the north of Burial 12, was also on the floor of House E^2. It was of the central-chamber variety. The shaft measured 3.9 x 4 feet across the top and was 1.6 feet deep. The chamber measured 2.8 feet wide and 3.7 feet long and was 1.5 feet deep. Just above the ledge, the wall was undercut, and the crevice contained the charred ends of several of the logs that had covered the burial chamber (Figure 16). The well-preserved skeletal remains were of a 22- to 27-year-old male. The body had been placed in the chamber in a loosely flexed position on its left side with the head to the west. The arms were positioned so that the left hand was under the mandible and the right hand was on the right side of the skull. There were columella bead bracelets at each wrist (seven large beads on the right arm and six smaller ones on the left arm). A columella ear pin was positioned at each temporal bone. The artifacts from Burial 13 are illustrated in Plate 57.

Burial 14:

This burial, also of the central-chamber variety, was located just to the west of House E. The shaft measured 3 x 4 feet across the top and 1.7 feet to the top of the slightly undercut chamber ledge. The floor of the chamber was 0.7 foot below the ledge. The poorly preserved skeletal remains were determined to be of a female, 18 to 25 years old. The body had been placed in the chamber on its back with the legs drawn up to the left side. The arms were loosely flexed with the hands at the knees, and the head was oriented to the west. There were no associated artifacts.

Burial 15:

This was a central-chamber burial located at the center of the floor of House E^2 (Plate 33). Partially overlying the pit were the remains of a platform hearth, represented by a plow-disturbed concentration of burnt clay. Remnants of an earlier hearth were found in the upper fill of the burial in the form of burnt clay, ash, and charcoal. The pit was rectangular in shape and measured 2.7 x 4.3 feet across the top and 1.7 feet to the chamber ledge. From the ledge to the floor of the chamber was another 1.2 feet. At the west end of the chamber, two large, flat stones had been propped against the wall behind the skull. A single stone had been similarly positioned at the east end of the chamber. These stones probably served as supports for the chamber covering. Undercut areas on the walls of the shaft just above the ledge also indicated that there had been a

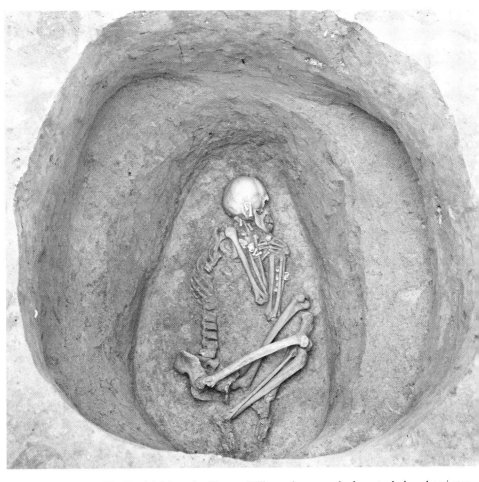

PLATE 32. Burial 13 at the Warren Wilson site, a typical central-chamber interment.

PLATE 33. Burial 15 at the Warren Wilson site.

covering. The body had been placed in the chamber on its left side with the legs flexed, elbows at the knees, hands under the head, and the head to the west. The bones were those of a 35- to 40-year-old female. A thin layer of decayed organic matter was found under the bones, possibly the residue of bark, cloth, or skins that had been placed on the floor of the chamber prior to the interment. In the area of the wrists and neck were 250 small tubular shell beads and 20 columella beads (Plate 56). Although there was some disturbance in this area, caused by the collapse of the chamber covering, it would appear that both the columella and tubular beads had been suspended from the neck.

Burial 16:
Burial 16 was located just outside of the wall pattern of House E[1] and a few feet south of Burial 14. The pit was of the central-chamber variety. The pit measured 3.3 x 4.3 feet across the top and was 1.3 feet deep. From the ledge to the floor was 1.6 feet. The body had been placed in the chamber on its right side with the legs loosely flexed, the right arm extended under the legs, and the head to the west. The bones were of a male, 35 to 40 years old. Near the left hand and just above the left knee was a large, poorly preserved conch shell bowl. Around the neck was a necklace of 20 columella beads, and at each ankle was a rattle made from a juvenile box turtle *(Terrapene carolina)* carapace filled with small round pebbles.

Burial 17:
This was a side-chamber burial on the floor of House F. The north edge of the shaft was intrusive through the south edge of Burial 18. Across the top, the shaft measured 2.5 x 2.9 feet, and it was 1.7 feet deep. The chamber, on the south side of the shaft, measured 1.4 feet from end to end, 1 foot from front to back, and 1 foot from ceiling to floor. The floor of the chamber was 0.5 foot below the floor of the shaft. At the opening of the chamber was a shallow trench that had served to anchor the lower portion of the chamber covering. Molds left by the ends of the logs were found in the bottom of the trench. The chamber contained the badly decomposed remains of an infant or newborn, sex undetermined. There were no grave goods.

Burial 18:
This burial, another of the side-chamber type, was located immediately north of and was partially intruded by Burial 17 (Plate 34). The shaft measured 3.2 x 2.6 feet across the top and was 1.6 feet deep. The chamber, on the southwest side of the shaft, measured 1.9 feet from end to end, 1.7 feet from front to back, and 1.2 feet from ceiling to floor. The floor of the chamber was 0.5 foot below the floor of the shaft. The opening of the chamber was covered by three large, flat river boulders (Plate 34). The fill behind the stones was dark and loose, but no skeletal re-

PLATE 34. Burial 18 at the Warren Wilson site, with rock covering in place.

mains were encountered. Probably, the burial had been of a newborn or infant and the bones had completely decomposed.

Burial 19:

Burial 19 (Figure 11; Plate 35) was at the center of the floor of House F. The burial pit was found in the bottom of a larger shallow pit (Feature 153) and under a prepared clay platform hearth (Feature 154). The fill of the shallow pit overlay the burial and contained ash, fragments of burnt clay, and part of a charred log. It appeared that Feature 153 had been dug by the inhabitants of House F for the purpose of removing an existing hearth, and then the pit for Burial 19 was dug in the position formerly occupied by the hearth. After the burial pit had been backfilled, a new hearth (Feature 154) was constructed, and the cavity around this hearth was then refilled with the debris from the old hearth.

Burial 19 was of the central-chamber variety. The top of the pit measured 4.1 x 5 feet. From the top (bottom of Feature 153) to the ledge was 1 foot, and from the ledge to the chamber floor was 1.5 feet. The chamber measured 3.3 x 4.3 feet. A lens of partially decomposed organic matter sloped downward from the ledge to just above the level of the bones. This was identified as bark and segments of river cane, probably the remains of the collapsed chamber covering. The skeletal remains, in a good state of preservation, belonged to a male, 20 to 25 years old. The body had been positioned on its left side with the arms and legs loosely flexed and the head to the west.

Burial 20:

Burial 20 also was located on the floor of House F, a few feet from Burials 17, 18, and 19. It was a side-chamber interment. The shaft was 2.4 feet in diameter and 0.9 foot deep. The chamber, on the south side of the shaft, measured 2.7 feet from end to end, 1.6 feet from front to back, and 1 foot from ceiling to floor. The floor of the chamber was 0.4 foot below the floor of the shaft. Logs had been propped against the opening of the chamber, as was evidenced by a shallow trench containing the end molds of several of these logs. There were no skeletal remains in the chamber, and it is probable that the interment was an infant or newborn and that the fragile bones had decomposed.

Burial 21:

Burial 21 was located just to the north of Burial 19 on the floor of House F. It was of the side-chamber variety. The shaft measured 3.7 feet long x 2.7 feet wide and was 1.6 feet deep. The chamber, located on the northwest side, measured 3 feet from side to side and 1.6 feet from front to back. The top of the chamber was truncated by plowing; the floor was 0.4 foot below the floor of the shaft. The remains of a newborn or infant were found in a small cluster in the middle of the chamber floor.

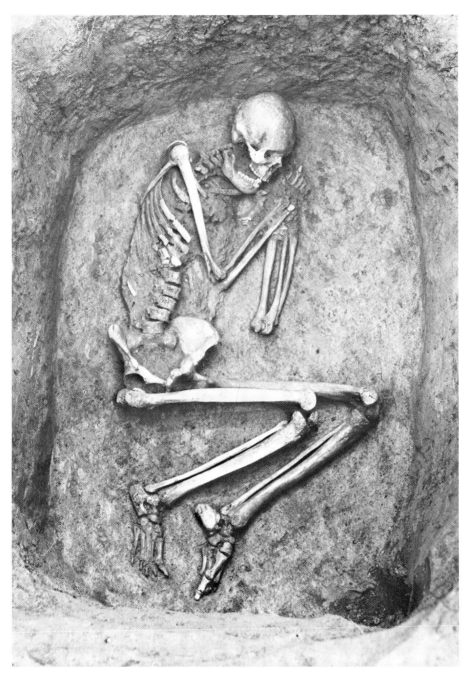

PLATE 35. Burial 19 at the Warren Wilson site.

Burial 22:

Burial 22, also on the floor of House F, was located a few feet northeast of Burial 19. It was of the central-chamber variety. The top of the pit measured 3.1 x 3.9 feet. It was 0.9 foot from the top of the pit to the ledge and 0.8 foot from the ledge to the floor of the chamber. The chamber measured 2 x 3.8 feet. The body had been placed in the chamber in a flexed position on its left side with the head to the west. The poorly preserved bones were of a male, 14 to 16 years old. No artifacts accompanied the burial.

Burial 23:

The pit for Burial 23 was found in the bottom of Feature 108, a large refuse-filled depression on the floor of House G (Plate 36). The simple burial pit measured 2.1 x 3.7 feet across the top and was 2.3 feet deeper than the bottom of the feature. The skeletal remains, poorly preserved, were determined to be of an adult 20 to 30 years of age, sex indeterminate. The body had been placed in the pit on its right side with the head to the west and the legs tightly flexed. There were no grave goods.

Burial 24:

This was a simple-pit interment located just outside of the southwest corner of House I. The pit measured 2.9 x 3.4 feet across the top and 3 feet deep. The skeletal remains were of a child, 3 to 6 years of age, sex indeterminate. Preservation was poor. The body had been placed on its left side with the arms and legs loosely flexed and the head to the southwest. There were no associated artifacts.

Burial 25:

This burial was located on the east side of the floor of House J. It was a simple pit that measured 2.5 x 3.5 feet across the top and 1.5 feet deep. The skeletal remains, poorly preserved, were of a 20- to 30-year-old male. The body had been positioned on its left side with the head to the west. The arms and legs were moderately flexed. There were no grave goods.

Burial 26:

This was a side-chamber burial located just outside of the southeast corner of House D. Because the roof of the chamber had completely collapsed, it was difficult to determine the size of the original shaft. It was estimated to have been about 2.6 feet in diameter and 0.6 foot deep. The chamber was on the north side and measured approximately 2.3 x 2.4 feet. The floor of the chamber was 0.6 foot below the floor of the shaft. The skeletal remains, located near the opening of the chamber, consisted of the bones of an infant or newborn, sex undetermined. Included with the burial was a highly decomposed shell gorget and a cluster of 36 perforated *Marginella* shells. The gorget was in the area of the skull, the shells adjacent to the pelvis.

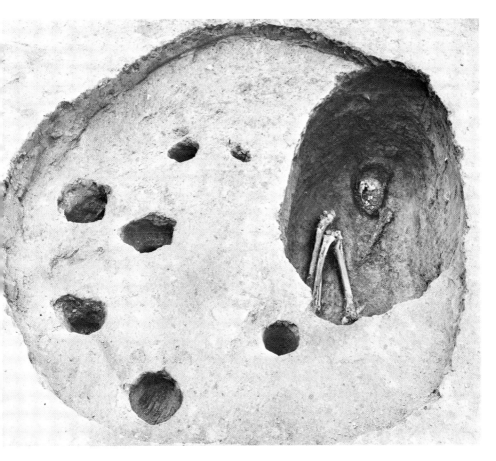

PLATE 36. Burial 23 and Feature 108 at the Warren Wilson site.

Burial 27:

This was a side-chamber burial located in the much eroded area east of Houses D and E and south of Houses B and C (Plate 37). The shaft measured 2.3 x 2.5 feet across the top and was 0.9 foot deep. The chamber measured 2.1 x 2.3 feet. The floor of the chamber was 0.3 foot below the floor of the shaft. A small cluster of skeletal remains, found in the northwest end of the chamber, were of an infant or newborn, sex undetermined. There were no grave goods.

Burial 28:

Burial 28 (Plate 37), another side-chamber interment, was located a few feet to the south of Burial 27. The shaft measured 3 x 4 feet across the top and was 0.9 foot deep. The chamber measured 2 x 4 feet and was 0.2 foot deeper than the shaft. The skeletal remains, poorly preserved, belonged to an adolescent, age 15 to 18 years, sex undetermined. The body had been placed in the chamber on its right side with the head to the west and the arms and legs loosely flexed. There were no associated artifacts.

Burial 29:

This was another side-chamber burial, located a few feet to the east of Burials 27 and 28 (Plate 37). The proximity of these three burials, and the similarity of the pits, makes it probable that they were members of the same household. Perhaps they were associated with a house structure, the post mold pattern for which had been obliterated through erosion. The shaft of the burial pit measured 3.4 x 2.2 feet across the top and was 1.5 feet deep. The chamber measured 2.2 x 3.2 feet, and its floor was 0.1 foot lower than the floor of the shaft. With the exception of the skull, which had been crushed by the collapse of the chamber roof, the skeletal remains were in a relatively good state of preservation. The remains were of an 18- to 20-year-old male. The body had been positioned on its back with the head to the southwest, the legs flexed to the left side, and the arms crossed over the chest. There was a turtle carapace rattle at each ankle.

Burial 30:

Burial 30 was found in the north-south exploratory trench, in the plaza area. The burial was in a simple pit that measured 3.3 x 2.6 feet across the top and 2 feet deep. The walls of the pit were vertical on the east and west sides, but were slightly undercut on the north and south sides. The skeletal remains, in a fair state of preservation, belonged to a female, 18 to 20 years of age. The body had been placed on its back, the head to the west, and the legs loosely flexed to the right side. The arms had been folded to each side with the hands on the shoulders. There were no grave goods.

Burial 31:

This was a simple-pit interment located just outside of the west wall of

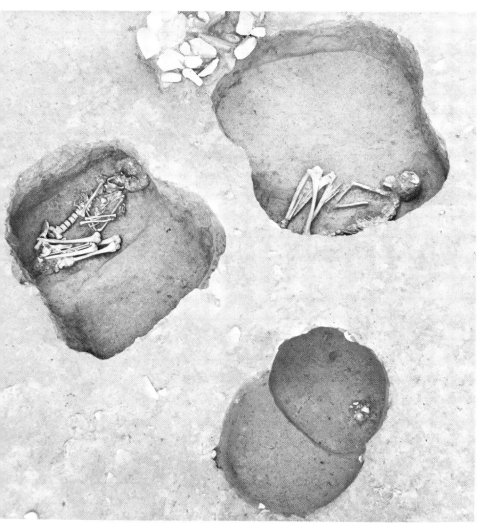

PLATE 37. Burials 27, 28 and 29 at the Warren Wilson site.

House I. Two post molds of the wall were intrusive through the edge of the burial pit. The pit measured 2.7 x 3.8 feet across the top and was 3.1 feet deep. The walls slanted inward slightly toward the bottom of the pit. The skeletal remains, poorly preserved, were determined to be a male, 38 to 45 years of age. The body had been placed in the grave on its left side, head to the west, with the arms and legs moderately flexed. No grave goods were present.

Burial 32:

This was a simple-pit burial located just southeast of House D. The pit measured 2.2 feet wide x 3.7 feet long and was 1.2 feet deep. The body had been placed in the pit on its right side in a loosely flexed position with the head to the west. The remains were of a male, 16 to 18 years of age. There were no artifact associations.

Burial 33:

Burial 33 (Figure 11; Plate 38) was located at the approximate center of the floor of House H. It was a side-chamber interment. The bottom portion of a basin-shaped clay hearth (Feature 140) overlay the burial pit (Plate 17). The shaft measured 3.4 x 3.8 feet across the top and was 2.7 feet deep. The chamber was on the south side of the shaft and measured 2.3 feet wide x 4.2 feet long and 1.6 feet from ceiling to floor. The floor of the chamber was 0.2 foot below the floor of the shaft. In front of the opening of the chamber, there was a shallow trench which contained marks made by the ends of at least eight logs used to cover the chamber. The linear molds of the logs themselves were discovered in the excavation of the shaft fill (Plate 39). The poorly preserved skeletal remains were of a young male, 14 to 16 years of age. The body had been placed in the chamber on its right side with the head to the west. The arms and legs were loosely flexed. Around the lower leg bones was found a group of 32 perforated rabbit bones *(Sylvilagus floridanus),* consisting of 16 innominate bones and 16 scapulae (Plate 52).

Burial 34:

Burial 34, a side-chamber interment, was located on the floor of House H, a few feet northeast of Burial 33. The shaft measured 1.9 x 2.1 feet across the top and was 0.8 foot deep. The collapsed chamber was 1.8 feet from front to back, 2.2 feet from end to end, and 1.4 feet deep. The bottom of the chamber was 0.7 foot deeper than the bottom of the shaft. A few teeth found on the west floor of the chamber were determined to be from an infant or newborn, sex undetermined. There were no grave goods.

Burial 35:

Burial 35, a simple-pit interment, was located adjacent to Burial 34. The pit was 1.9 feet wide, 2.7 feet long, and 1.6 feet deep. A thin lens of dark organic material in the bottom of the pit indicated that bones had once

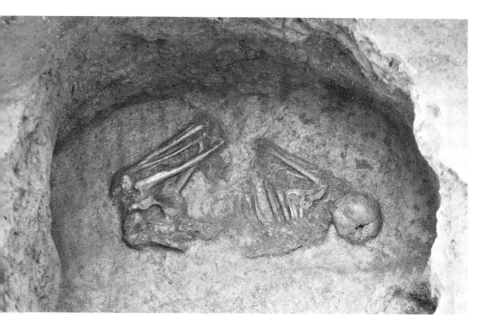

PLATE 38. Burial 33 at the Warren Wilson site.

PLATE 39. Log molds over the chamber in Burial 33 at the Warren Wilson site.

been present. From the size of the pit, it is suspected that the remains were of an infant or young child. There were no grave goods.

PATTERNING IN THE WARREN WILSON BURIALS[2]

Burials at the Warren Wilson site usually were grouped in the areas of house floors. Several seemingly isolated burials may have been associated with houses for which post mold patterns could not be defined. Of the 35 burials recovered by the close of the 1968 season, 14 were in simple pits, 14 were in side-chamber pits, and 7 were in central-chamber pits. The central-chamber burials all were associated with Houses E and F. House E was located within the area enclosed by Palisades B, C, D, E, and F and probably can be considered an earlier house than those that overlay the palisades. Although House F seemed to intrude on Palisades B, C, D, and E, it still could be earlier than Houses A, B, and C. This information, together with the fact that only one side-chamber burial was found in the area enclosed by Palisades B, C, D, E, and F, leads to the postulation that the central-chamber pit was earlier than, and possibly developmental to, the side-chamber pit. The simple pit form, found in all areas of excavation, probably was used concurrently with both of the chamber forms. Since only one out of fourteen burials in simple pits contained grave goods, it may be suggested that this was a less formal type of receptacle for persons of lower status or rank. Both males and females were found in central-chamber pits and simple pits, but only males were found in side-chamber pits.

There is abundant evidence that both the central and side chambers were sealed prior to refilling of the pits. In most cases, logs, or possibly logs covered with bark sheets or cane matting, were used for this purpose, although in one instance three large, flat stones were used to seal the mouth of a side chamber. In another case, stones had been employed at either end of a central chamber to aid in the support of a log covering.

There were five instances of interment beneath the hearth in the center of a house floor. Four of the five were chamber burials; the fifth was in a simple pit. Three were males and two were females. Before the digging of the pit for Burial 19 (House F), an old hearth was removed, and following the interment a new hearth was con-

2. A summary listing of traits for the Warren Wilson burials is provided in Table 2.

Table 2. Burials at the Warren Wilson Site.

Burial	House	Pit Type	Position	Heading	Sex	Age	Deformation	Grave Associations
1	A	Simple pit	Flexed on back	SE	F	30-35	Medium	None
2	A	Simple pit	Flexed on left side	NW	M	40-50	Pronounced	None
3	B2	Simple pit	?	?	?	-6 mos.	?	None
4	A2	Simple pit	Flexed on left side	W	?	3-6	?	None
5	B2	Simple pit	?	?	?	1/2-2	?	4 shell gorgets and Marginella shells
6	B2	Side chamber	?	?	?	-6 mos.	?	Tubular shell beads
7	B2	Side chamber	Flexed on back	W	M	35-40	Pronounced	Columella bracelets, conch shell, bone awls, ochre, fish scales, mica discs, and panther claws
8	B2	Simple pit	Flexed on back	W	F	25-30	Medium	None
9	C	Side chamber	?	?	?	-6 mos.	?	Columella beads and shell gorget
10	C?	Simple pit	Flexed on right side	W	M	23-28	Pronounced	None
11	C?	Side chamber	Flexed on back?	W	?	5-10	?	None
12	E2	Central chamber	?	?	?	-6 mos.	?	6 tubular shell beads
13	E2	Central chamber	Flexed on left side	W	M	25-30	Pronounced	Columella bead bracelets and shell ear pins
14	E?	Central chamber	Flexed on back	W	F	18-25	Pronounced	None
15	E2	Central chamber	Flexed on left side	W	F	35-40	Pronounced	Columella bead necklace and tubular shell bead necklace
16	E?	Central chamber	Flexed on right side	W	M	35-40	Pronounced	Columella bead necklace, two turtle shell rattles, and conch bowl
17	F	Side chamber	?	?	?	-6 mos.	?	None
18	F	Side chamber	?	?	?	-6 mos.	?	None
19	F	Central chamber	Flexed on left side	W	M	20-25	Medium	None
20	F	Side chamber	?	?	?	-6 mos.	?	None
21	F	Side chamber	?	?	?	-6 mos.	?	None
22	F	Central chamber	Flexed on left side	W	M	14-16	?	None
23	G	Simple pit	Flexed on right side	W	?	20-30	?	None
24	I?	Simple pit	Flexed on left side	SW	?	3-6	?	None
25	J	Simple pit	Flexed on left side	W	M	20-30	Pronounced	None
26	D?	Side chamber	?	?	?	-6 mos.	?	Marginella shells and shell gorget
27	?	Side chamber	?	?	?	-6 mos.	?	None
28	?	Side chamber	Flexed on right side	W	?	14-18	?	2 turtle shell rattles
29	?	Side chamber	Flexed on back	SW	?	18-20	?	None
30	?	Simple pit	Flexed on back	W	F	20-25	Slight	None
31	I?	Simple pit	Flexed on left side	W	M	40-45	Pronounced	None
32	D?	Simple pit	Flexed on right side	W	M	16-18	Pronounced	None
33	H	Side chamber	Flexed on right side	NW	M	14-16	Pronounced	Perforated rabbit bones
34	H	Side chamber	?	?	?	-6 mos.	?	None
35	H	Simple pit	?	?	?	-6 mos.?	?	None

structed directly over the burial pit in approximately the same location as the old hearth.

Of the 22 burials for which heading (orientation of the superior axis of the skeleton) could be determined (usually the heading of infant and child burials could not be determined), 17 (77 percent) were positioned with the head to the west, 2 (9 percent) to the northwest, 2 (9 percent) to the southwest, and 1 (5 percent) to the southeast (Table 2). This sample shows a strong bias for a westward orientation. These orientations correspond roughly to the directional distribution of other Pisgah sites when viewed from the Warren Wilson site. That is, over 70 percent of the recorded Pisgah sites lie to the west, southwest, or northwest of the Warren Wilson site, while less than 30 percent lie to the north, northeast, east, southeast, or south. Of the 70 percent having a westward location, the largest concentration (including the important mound center at Garden Creek) is on the upper Pigeon drainage, on a line a few degrees south of due west (Figure 2).

Artificial deformation was observed on all sufficiently preserved adult crania from the Warren Wilson site. This was of the fronto-parieto-occipital variety, which Neumann (1942:309) found "to be confined to the territory occupied by the Cherokee in northern Georgia, eastern Tennessee, and western North Carolina." Of the 15 deformed skulls, the degree of deformation was pronounced on 11, medium on 3, and slight on 1.

Of the 17 skeletons on which sex determinations could be made, there were 12 males and 5 females. An age estimation was made for all 35 burials, of which 12 were less than 6 months, 4 were from 6 months to 10 years, 5 were from 10 to 20 years, 8 were from 20 to 30 years, 4 were from 30 to 40 years, and 2 were from 40 to 50 years.

Grave accompaniments were present (or at least were well enough preserved to be recognized) in 11 of 35 burials. In nine burials, the artifacts were ornamental. These consisted of shell beads, shell gorgets, shell ear pins, mica discs, turtle shell rattles, and perforated animal bones. Columella beads worn as either bracelets or necklaces were most common. Two burials contained nonornamental artifacts; one had a conch shell bowl, the other a small conch shell, two bone awls, and a cache of red ocher, garfish scales, and six panther claws. Of the 17 sexed burials, 5 of 12 males and 1 of 5 females had grave accompaniments. Shell gorgets were found only with infants or young children. Three out of five burials on the floor of House B and four out of five burials in the vicinity of House E had accompanying artifacts. On the other hand, none of the burials associated with Houses A and F had artifacts. Even Burial 19 (House F), which had received considerable attention in the preparation and placement of the burial pit, contained no grave goods.

On the basis of this small burial sample, it would appear that males were more commonly buried in chambered pits and with ornamentation than were females. Except for the shell gorgets, age had little to do with determining the disposition of grave artifacts. Neither does degree of cranial deformation seem to have been related to the presence or absence of grave goods. There does appear to have been a difference in the use of grave goods by family or household units. This may indicate differential ranking among kin groups in the community, or it may only reflect temporal variation in burial customs. The fact that sumptuary items, especially beads and gorgets, were included with infants and young children may suggest that ranking followed hereditary lines (Larson 1971:67). The two occurrences of turtle shell rattles were with adult males. This is interesting in the light of the fact that early observers among the Southeastern Indians always reported such rattles as being worn by females (e.g., Adair 1775:101, 116, 178). Burial 7 contained an uncommon abundance of grave goods, including some items found in no other burials on the site (mica discs, red ocher, and panther claws). It is probable that this older male was a high-ranking individual, or possibly a shaman.

GARDEN CREEK MOUNDS 1 AND 2

Twenty-three burials were found in the excavations at Garden Creek Mound No. 1.[3] Three were intrusive through the toe of the mound, three originated at the level of premound humus, and the remaining seventeen originated on one of the floor or fill stages. Four other burials were found in a house floor in the village area east of the mound. All these burials were judged to be of Pisgah affiliation, although most of the mound burials appear to have been

---

3. A summation of the data on these burials is provided in Table 3.

Table 3. Burials at the Garden Creek Site.

Burial	Provenience	Pit Type	Heading	Sex	Age	Grave Associations
Mound No. 1 and Village						
1	Intrusive toe of mound	Simple pit	W	F	Adult	Tubular shell beads and a shell ear pin
2	Intrusive toe of mound	Simple pit	SE	?	Juvenile	None
3	Below Floor 2	Side chamber	NW	?	Juvenile	1 shell gorget and tubular shell beads
4	Below Floor 2	Side chamber	E	?	Juvenile	Columella beads and tubular shell beads
5	Floor 2	Simple pit	N	?	Adult	None
6	Below Floor 2	Side chamber	SW	?	1-3	Tubular shell beads and 6 shell gorgets
7	Below Floor 2	Simple pit	?	?	Infant	Columella beads and tubular shell beads
8	Below Floor 2	Side chamber	NW	?	Juvenile	Shell gorget and columella beads
9	Below Floor 2	Simple pit	?	?	Infant	None
10	?	Simple pit	SE	?	Juvenile	None
11	?	Simple pit	NW	M	18-20	Columella beads and 3 stone discs
12	?	Simple pit	E	?	3-5	1 shell bead
13	?	Simple pit	W	?	12-15	Tubular shell beads and shell gorget
14	?	Simple pit	N	?	Adult?	None
15	?	Simple pit	S	?	4-6	Tubular shell beads and 2 shell gorgets
16	Intrusive mound fill	Simple pit	SE	?	40-50	Conch bowl
17	Intrusive mound fill	Simple pit	NW	M	40-50	1 shell bead
18	Intrusive Floor 3	Simple pit	N	?	?	1 turtle shell rattle?
19	HWV7 (1)	Simple pit	NW	M	Adolescent	None
20	HWV7 (2)	Side chamber	?	?	Infant	None
21	HWV7 (3)	Side chamber	W	?	6-8	None
22	HWV7 (4)	Simple pit	NW	F	Adult	1 shell gorget
23	Floor 1-A	Simple pit	NW	F	Adult	None
24	Pre-mound humus	Simple pit	?	?	Adult	2 stone celts
25	Intrusive toe of mound	Simple pit	?	?	Infant	None
26	Pre-mound humus	Simple pit	?	?	?	None
27	Pre-mound humus	Simple pit	N	M	28-32	None
Mound No. 2						
1	Mound Stage 2	Simple pit	?	?	Infant	1 shell bead
2	Intrusive mound	Simple pit	?	?	Infant	2 Marginella shells, 2 disc beads and 1 shell gorget
3	Mound Stage 2	Simple pit	W	?	14-16	None
4	?	Simple pit?	?	?	Juvenile	None
5	Intrusive mound	Side chamber	NW	F	Adult	None
6	Mound Stage 2	Side chamber	S	?	Adult	Shell beads
7	Mound Stage 2	Simple pit	W	M	Adult	None
8	Mound Stage 1	Simple pit	E	M	Adolescent	None

late in the Pisgah phase (ca. A.D. 1350-1450).

There were 6 side-chamber and 21 simple-pit burials. The central-chamber pit was absent, which lends support to the early placement of this type of burial pit. The number of infant burials was fewer at Garden Creek Mound No. 1 than at Warren Wilson. Otherwise, the proportions of age groups were similar. Preservation was generally poorer at Garden Creek, and only eight burials were identified as to sex—four males and four females.

All of the burials were flexed. Nine (33 percent) were positioned with the head to the northwest, five (18 percent) to the west, one (4 percent) to the southwest, two (8 percent) to the south, three (11 percent) to the southeast, three (11 percent) to the east, none to the northeast, and four (15 percent) to the north. Although this distribution is more random than at Warren Wilson, a generally western heading—15 out of 27 burials (55 percent)—is indicated. The Garden Creek site is located just southeast of the centroid of Pisgah site distribution.

The most common grave accompaniments were columella beads, tubular shell beads, shell gorgets, and shell ear pins. One burial contained a conch shell bowl, another had a turtle shell rattle, one had a cache of three ground stone discs, and one had two ground stone celts. The inclusion of ground stone artifacts in burials is a trait of the succeeding Qualla phase and probably represents a late addition to Pisgah burial practices.

Grave goods were found in just over half of the burials at Mound No. 1, as compared with only 30 percent at the Warren Wilson village site. Such a difference may indicate higher rank for the individuals buried in the mound, and it is unfortunate that there is not an adequate comparative sample of village burials from the Garden Creek site. Although grave goods were somewhat more numerous at Garden Creek Mound No. 1, they did not differ in form (except for the celts and discs) or in quantity per burial from those at the Warren Wilson site.

Eight Pisgah burials were intrusive through Stages 1 or 2 at Garden Creek Mound No. 2.[4] Six of these burials were in simple pits, and two were in side-chamber pits. Three of them contained grave goods.

---

4. For a summary list of traits, see Table 3.

PISGAH BURIALS AT OTHER SITES

A single Pisgah burial was excavated at the Rankin site on the French Broad River in Cocke County, Tennessee (David Smith, personal communication). It was the burial of a child, sex undetermined and age estimated at 6 years. The simple pit was 2.2 feet in diameter at the top and 1.8 feet deep. The skeleton was on its right side, flexed, with the head to the northwest. A small Pisgah Plain vessel with collared rim (Smith and Hodges 1968:Plate 44) was inverted next to the skull. This is the only known instance of the inclusion of a ceramic vessel in a Pisgah burial.

Several burials of Pisgah affiliation were found at the I. C. Few site on the Keowee River in northwestern South Carolina. The archaeologist (Roger Grange, personal communication) described these burials as being "in pits, flexed, usually without artifacts but sometimes with shell beads or discs."

AREAL AND TEMPORAL RELATIONSHIPS

An examination of other cultures in the Southern Appalachians on a comparable time level to Pisgah reveals some widespread similarities in burial traits. For example, the placing of burials in or adjacent to houses, as opposed to village cemeteries, is reported for the Dallas phase of eastern Tennessee (Lewis and Kneberg 1946: 143), for the Wilbanks phase of north-central Georgia (Larson 1971:66), and for the Barnett phase (Dallas-Lamar) in northwestern Georgia (Garrow and Smith 1973:5-10).

Central-chamber burials have been found on sites of the Dallas phase (Lewis and Kneberg 1946:144; Webb 1938:179), the Wilbanks and Barnett phases (A. R. Kelly, personal communication), and the Woodside phase of southeastern Kentucky (Dunnell, Hanson, and Hardesty 1971:35-40). Side-chamber burials have been reported for the Barnett phase (Patrick Garrow, personal communication), the Woodside phase (Dunnell, Hanson, and Hardesty 1971: 35-40), the Pee Dee phase on the Carolina Piedmont (Joffre Coe, personal communication), and in one instance for the Wilbanks phase at the Etowah site in north Georgia (Lewis Larson, personal communication).

At the Slone site (Woodside phase) in Kentucky, the three burial pit types—simple pit, side chamber, and central chamber—were present together in a village of similar size and organization to the Warren Wilson site. There were some differences at the Slone site, in that the central-chamber type was the most common (49 percent), stone slabs were usually employed as chamber coverings, and many of the interments were extended (which would have affected the size and form of the pit).

The placing of hearths over burial pits, as was noted in five cases at the Warren Wilson site, has a few possible counterparts at other sites. Burial 17 in Mound Stage 1 at the Chauga site, South Carolina, lay partly beneath a platform hearth (Kelly and Neitzel 1961:12), a burial at the Cox site on the Clinch River in Tennessee had an overlying clay hearth basin (Myers 1961:22-25), and the remains of a "redeposited fire" was found over a burial (Feature 31) at the Slone site, Kentucky (Dunnell, Hanson, and Hardesty 1971:24-25). In none of the above cases could it be determined that the burial was located in the center of a house floor.

In western North Carolina, ample evidence exists for the continuity of Pisgah burial practices into the Qualla phase. For example, burials under house floors, the use of simple and side-chamber pits, and even one burial in a chambered pit under the central hearth of a house have been reported for an early 18th-century Qualla component at the Coweeta Creek site in Macon County (Runquist 1970; Joffre Coe, personal communication). Burials at this site also contained shell artifacts either identical to or in the same stylistic continuum as those found in Pisgah burials (see Chapter 4). Such continuities in burial practices may represent the strongest evidence for a religious and ideological tradition that persisted from Pisgah to Qualla, and thus from the prehistoric cultures to the historic Cherokees.

4. Artifacts

Artifacts recovered from the Pisgah sites are varied in materials and form, and along with ceramics,[1] offer the most significant body of comparative data. I have grouped these artifacts into five categories, according to the material from which they were made—stone, clay, bone, shell, and wood.[2] The absolute quantity and diversity of remains within each of these categories are heavily biased by differential preservation, an important consideration since preservation of organic materials is poor on open sites in the Southeast.

In this chapter, the artifacts from the Warren Wilson site are described in greatest detail, and this information is supplemented with information from Garden Creek and other sites. Particular artifact forms and stylistic attributes are compared with those recorded for contemporaneous cultures in neighboring portions of the South Appalachian province. The Pisgah artifact assemblage is also compared with earlier and later assemblages in the Appalachian Summit, placing special emphasis on the position of Pisgah in the development of Cherokee material culture.

STONE ARTIFACTS

Stone artifacts fall into four broad categories that reflect technique of manufacture or use modification. These are chipped stone, ground stone, pecked stone, and cut stone. Obviously, some stone tools were subjected to more than one of the manipulations implied by the above classifications. For example, a celt might first have been roughly pecked into shape, later to be ground on all or part of its surface. Since the resulting celt was always at least partly ground, it is classed as a ground stone tool.

1. Pottery sherds, the most common type of artifact in all contexts, were quantitatively and stylistically the most amenable to analysis and are treated separately in Ch. 5.
2. Table 4 lists all artifacts recovered from the pit fill of Pisgah features and burials.

Table 4. Artifacts in Feature and Burial Pitfill at the Warren Wilson Site.

	Chipped Stone Projectile Point	Flake Tool	Flint Core	Ground Stone Celt	Ground Stone Disc	Polishing Stone	Mortar	Anvil Stone	Mano	Hammerstone	Cut Mica	Pigment Stone	Clay Disc	Clay Pipe	Clay Bead	Clay Miniature Pot	Bone Tool	Shell Bead
Feature																		
4	3																	
6	1									2								
7	2				1		1			1			3	6			3	
9							1			1								
14	1																	
37							1			1				1				
40	1			1														
47	1				1						1		1				1	15
53											2							13
54		1					1											
55	1													1				
56																		1
57	4	3	1	1	3			1				1		2	2		11	16
85			1					1	1									
86		2									7			1		2		
107	1	2								2								
108	1												1					
136	2	2			2					1				2	1			
137	1	1															1	3
140								1		1				3				
Burial																		
1	2																1	1
3							1			1							2	
7	1																	
8	5													1			1	
11	2																	
12				1														
13	1													1				
14		3																
15		1				1												
16	1																	
18		2			1													
19	2							1						1			2	
21											1							
22	1	1								1				1				
24	1	1																
25	1																	
26	3																	
27	1																	
28		1								1		1						
Totals	40	20	1	2	9	1	5	3	2	11	11	1	5	20	3	2	22	49

CHIPPED STONE

Most Pisgah chipped stone artifacts were fashioned from small flakes of chert (black, gray, or tan), milky quartz, quartzite, or slate. Some of the cherts were obtained from local sources, while others probably came from eastern Tennessee or northern Georgia. Quartz and quartzite pebbles were present in any local stream bed, and the metamorphosed slate probably was acquired from the Uwarrie Hills area of the North Carolina Piedmont.

The characteristic projectile point (presumably an arrow tip) of the Pisgah phase is a small isosceles or equilateral triangle manufactured on a flake of one of the above materials (Plate 40). Some of these points exhibit careful bifacial flaking and are symmetrical in outline and of even thickness, but more often a flake was only moderately retouched to achieve a roughly triangular form. The bases are either straight, concave, or slightly convex. The lateral edges are sometimes serrated.

A sample of 30 relatively complete points from various contexts at the Warren Wilson site were examined in detail. In this sample, the materials in order of frequency were black chert, gray chert, tan chert, quartz, quartzite, and slate. The lengths ranged from 16 to 30 mm, with a mean length of 24.5 mm. Widths (across the base) were from 11 to 21 mm, with a mean width of 15 mm. Points with straight to slightly convex bases were twice as numerous as those with concave bases.

Collectively, these points are indistinguishable in form and technique of manufacture from those found in many Late Woodland and Mississippian contexts in the Eastern Woodlands. Because of the frequent lack of careful retouching and the presence of serrated edges, they resemble rather closely points reported for Dallas sites in eastern Tennessee (Webb 1938:Plates 64, 66, 81). Also, a very comparable collection of points is described and illustrated for the Woodside component at the Slone site in southeastern Kentucky (Dunnell, Hanson, and Hardesty 1971:49-53 and Figures 31-33).

A second category of chipped stone consists of a variety of small retouched flakes, with edges prepared for cutting, scraping, sawing, boring, or graving. At the Warren Wilson site, 20 such tools were recovered from feature and burial fill, and a number of others were found in the general midden. The 20 specimens from pit fill contexts were examined in detail (Plate 41). All of these were made on

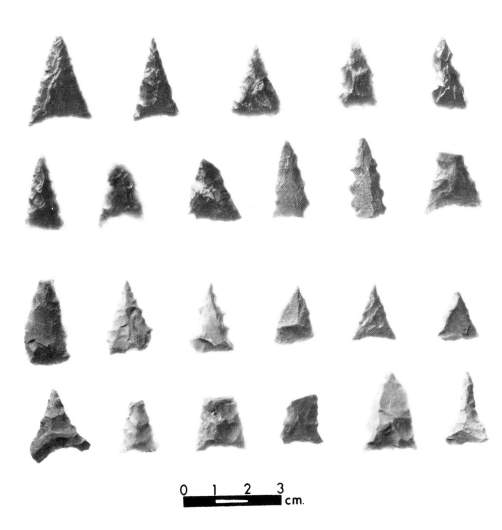

PLATE 40. Selection of chipped stone projectile points from the Warren Wilson site.

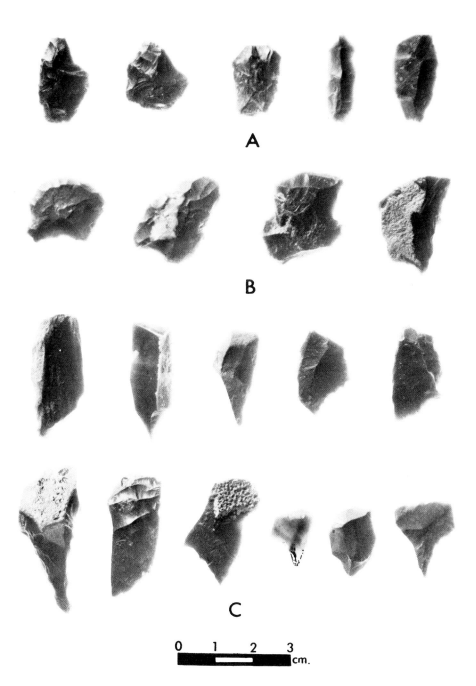

PLATE 41. Selection of flake tools from the Warren Wilson site. A, cutting tools; B, scrapers; C, boring and graving tools.

flakes of gray or black chert. In most cases a single-use classification was not possible. Of the twenty tools, eight had a cutting edge and a graving or boring point; one had a graving point, a straight cutting edge, and a concave cutting edge; one had a graving point, a concave cutting edge, and a scraping edge; one had a straight cutting edge and a concave cutting edge; one had a graving point and a scraping edge; five had only graving points; and one had only a "drill"-type point. These tools probably were used in various tasks associated with hide preparation, woodworking, and the carving and engraving of bone and shell. Most of them probably were hafted, while others may have been hand-held.

These small retouched and utilized flakes, which seem to be an important component of the Pisgah artifact assemblage, are not commonly reported for surrounding cultures. This may be due, at least in part, to a lack of recognition of these as tools or to a low estimation of their importance. One comparable set of flake tools, which included "scrapers," "knives," "gravers," "piercing tools," and "drills," is reported for the Woodside component at the Slone site, Pike County, Kentucky (Dunnell, Hanson, and Hardesty 1971: 46-48).

Several small chert cores, which presumably provided the flakes for the above-described tools and points, were found in the Warren Wilson excavations. Some of these exhibited prepared striking platforms, whereas others were simply small nodules that had been partly trimmed and discarded.

GROUND STONE

Two celt fragments, one each from Features 40 and 57, were found in feature pit fill at the Warren Wilson site, and two complete specimens, one of peridotite and the other of slate (Plate 42), were found in Burial 25 at Garden Creek Mound No. 1. Several additional specimens came from the general midden at the Warren Wilson and Garden Creek sites. The basic form of all of these celts was rectangular, with the bit end somewhat wider than the butt end, and with a slightly biconvex cross section. Some specimens were roughly pecked, with only the bits being ground, while others were ground all over. On a few specimens the butt ends were battered, suggesting that they had been used as hammers. Materials for these celts consisted of various mafic igneous rocks having textures ranging from diorite-gabbro to diabase. One small ground stone tool,

0 1 2 3
cm.

PLATE 42. Ground stone celts. A and B from Burial 25 at Garden Creek Mound No. 1; C, small celt with beveled bit from Warren Wilson site.

possibly a reworked broken celt, had a beveled (chisel?) bit (Plate 42).

Rectangular celts have been reported by Lewis and Kneberg (1946:120 and Plate 71) for the Dallas component at Hiwassee Island; by Webb (1938:Plates 64, 104) for several sites in the Norris Basin; by Wauchope (1966:Figure 114) for Mississippian sites on the Etowah and upper Chattahoochee rivers; and by Dunnell, Hanson, and Hardesty (1971:57-58) for the Slone site. Lewis and Kneberg consider the rectanguloid form to be a diagnostic trait of the Dallas phase, distinct from the thicker, rounder form of the Hiwassee Island phase (Lewis and Kneberg 1946:118-120).

Small ground stone discs (Plate 43) commonly occurred in Pisgah contexts. Nine of these were found in feature and burial fill at the Warren Wilson site, and three well-shaped and highly ground specimens were found in Burial 11 at Garden Creek Mound No. 1. These discs were made from a variety of materials, including diorite, diabase, gneiss, schist, and steatite. They ranged from 1.5 to 6 cm in diameter and from 5 to 15 mm in thickness. They usually were flat-sided, but an occasional biconvex specimen was noted. The degree of finishing varied from roughly formed pieces (some of these may have been unfinished) to carefully ground and symmetrical specimens.

Stone discs are found in numerous Mississippian contexts in the Southeast, but they seem to be especially abundant in collections from sites in the South Appalachian province. Lewis and Kneberg (1946:121-122) related them specifically to the Dallas component at Hiwassee Island, Wauchope (1966:188) found them exclusively in mature Mississippian contexts in northern Georgia, and Dunnell, Hanson, and Hardesty (1971:60-62 and Plate 38) found them with the Woodside component in eastern Kentucky.

Several flat river pebbles having a high polish on one or both surfaces were found in Pisgah contexts (Plate 44G-I). Such pieces probably were used as pottery burnishing tools. A single polished stone pipe, probably of steatite, was found on the surface at the Warren Wilson site (Plate 46, upper left). This specimen was quite similar in form to clay pipes from definite Pisgah contexts at the same site.

PECKED STONE

Pecked stone mortars, anvil stones, manos, and hammerstones

PLATE 43. Selection of ground stone discs from the Warren Wilson site.

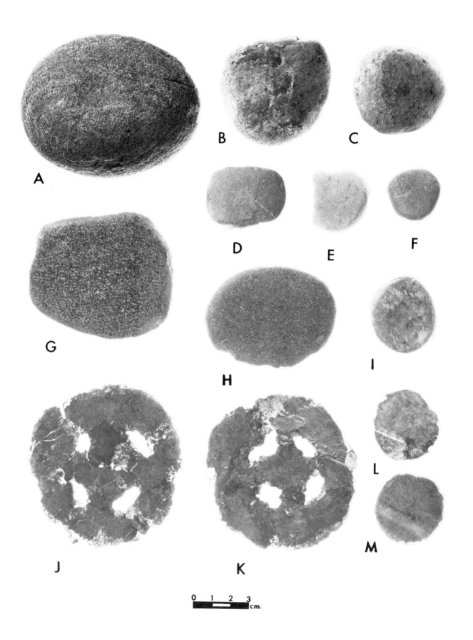

0 1 2 3 cm.

PLATE 44. Pecked, polished, and cut stone artifacts from the Warren Wilson site. A, B, and C, large hammerstones; D, E, and F, small hammerstones; G, H, and I, polishing stones; J-M, cut mica discs from Burial 7.

were found in Pisgah contexts at both the Warren Wilson and the Garden Creek sites. Five mortars—slab-shaped boulders having one or more abraded areas or shallow depressions—were found in the feature and burial fill at the Warren Wilson site. These probably were used as platforms for grinding vegetables or mineral pigments. Three smaller pebbles having one or more shallow pecked depressions were classed as anvil stones. A function as nut- or seed-cracking platforms is proposed.

River pebbles with one or more abraded surfaces were classed as manos. Two of these tools were recovered in feature pit fill at the Warren Wilson site. Such pieces probably were used with the above-described mortars to grind vegetables or mineral pigments.

Hammerstones were the most numerous artifact in the pecked stone category. Eleven of these tools were found in feature and burial pit fill at the Warren Wilson site. There appeared to be two major groups in this category. In one group (Plate 44A-C), the stones (usually water-worn pebbles) were about fist-size and had heavy mutilations on several surfaces (sometimes these had also doubled as anvils). In a second group (Plate 44D-F), the pebbles were smaller (about golf-ball-size) and had finer peck marks, usually restricted to a small area on the stone. The larger, rougher hammers probably were employed in primary stone working and for crushing seeds and nutshells, whereas the smaller hammers probably were used for secondary flint working.

Mortars, anvil stones, manos, and hammerstones have a broad temporal and geographical distribution in the Eastern Woodlands.

CUT STONE

Small fragments of cut mica were found in the pit fill and plow zone at both the Warren Wilson and the Garden Creek sites, and finished mica ornaments were present in one burial at the Warren Wilson site. It appears that the raw material was obtained in large irregular sheets at the quarries and was later worked into "preforms" or finished artifacts at the habitation sites. Evidence of aboriginal mica mining was found by geologists and mining engineers in the western North Carolina area in the late 19th and early 20th centuries (Ferguson n.d.). It is probable that local mica was exported by the Pisgah peoples, perhaps in exchange for such exotic materials as marine shells and chert.

The finished mica ornaments were found with Burial 7 (Plate 54) at the Warren Wilson site. They consisted of fifteen small solid discs (Plate 44L, M) and two small excised discs in the neck area and six large excised discs (Plate 44J, K) in the chest and abdominal areas. The excised specimens had four slots cut out to form a crude cross motif somewhat reminiscent of the circular rattlesnake gorgets from other burials at the same site.

Cut mica discs seem to have a rather restricted distribution in the Southeast. Two examples, one ring-shaped and the other a solid disc, were found with the Dallas component at Hiwassee Island, Tennessee (Lewis and Kneberg 1946:123 and Plate 75). Two discs with cutout sections identical to those from the Warren Wilson site were found with a burial of the Pee Dee phase at the Town Creek site, North Carolina (Joffre Coe, personal communication), and another similar specimen was found at the McCollum Mound (Pee Dee phase) in Chester County, South Carolina (Smithsonian Institution, Museum of Natural History, photograph 37318-E).

Pieces of cut or abraded "soft" minerals were present in various Pisgah contexts at the Warren Wilson and Garden Creek sites. Hematite, limonite, and graphite have been identified. A cache of ground red ocher was found with Burial 7 at the Warren Wilson site.

CLAY ARTIFACTS

Artifacts of fired clay consisted of discs, smoking pipes, animal head effigies, beads, and miniature pots. Clay discs were the most numerous item in this category (Plate 45). In most cases, these were made from a potsherd that had been chipped to a roughly circular form and then ground on the edges to produce a symmetrical disc. Rarely, the piece was fashioned from wet clay and fired. Sizes ranged from 1 to 5 cm in diameter and were from 4 to 9 mm thick. Such discs, probably used as gaming or counting pieces, have been found in a variety of late prehistoric contexts in the Southeast. In the Southern Appalachians, for example, they have been reported for the Dallas phase in eastern Tennessee (Lewis and Kneberg 1946: 106), the mature Mississippian phases in northern Georgia (Wauchope 1966:189, 191), the Irene and Savannah components at the Irene site, Chatham County, Georgia (Caldwell and McCann 1941: 53, 75 and Plate 18), and the Woodside phase in southeastern Kentucky (Dunnell, Hanson, and Hardesty 1971:60-62 and Plates 37, 44).

Clay smoking pipes were fairly numerous in Pisgah contexts at

PLATE 45. Selection of clay discs from the Warren Wilson site.

both the Warren Wilson and the Garden Creek sites. At Warren Wilson, 20 whole or fragmentary pipes were found in the feature and burial fill (Plate 46). These were small elbow pipes on which the stems usually were slightly shorter than the bowls, and the bowls were flared or rimmed at the top and usually decorated with ridges, incised lines, or nodes. Some had highly burnished surfaces, while others were only lightly smoothed. A heavy cake of burnt organic material was present in most of the intact bowls.

There are close similarities in form and decoration of these pipes to ones found on sites of the same general time period in neighboring portions of the Southeast. Note should be taken of the pipes illustrated for the Dallas component at Hiwassee Island, Tennessee (Lewis and Kneberg 1946:106 and Plate B except for the bottom right piece), for "large-log town house" (Dallas phase) contexts in the Norris Basin of eastern Tennessee (Webb 1938:Plates 67a and 81a), for the mature Mississippian (Etowah and Wilbanks) phases in northern Georgia (Wauchope 1966:Figures 139, 254), for sites of the Pee Dee phase on the Carolina Piedmont (Coe 1952:Figure 165), and for the Savannah and Irene phases on the Georgia-South Carolina Coastal Plain (Caldwell and McCann 1941:Plate 18).

Twelve small clay animal heads were found in the plow zone at the Warren Wilson site (Plate 47A-H, K), and were presumed to be associated with the Pisgah phase occupation. There was one complete animal, possibly a bear effigy (Plate 47, I), while the others were heads only (each was broken at the base of the neck). These appear to be simple representations of deer. It is not known to what these heads were attached, since no whole figures (other than the bear) were found. It is possible that they were pot rim appendages, although no such rims were noted in the sherd analyses.

Forty-four clay beads were recovered in the Warren Wilson excavations, and a few similar specimens were found at the Garden Creek site (Plate 48). The forms were spherical, oblong, elongated with expanded center, spool-shaped, and pear-shaped. The spherical and oblong forms were the most common, with a range in diameter (or greatest dimension) of 5 to 15 mm. Clay beads were never included as burial accompaniments, which would lead to an interpretation of their use as "casual" ornamentation, either suspended individually, strung, or sewn to garments. Spherical and oblong clay beads have been reported by Lewis and Kneberg (1946:106 and Plate 64) for the Dallas component at Hiwassee Island, by Wauchope (1966:207 and Figure 253) for the Wilbanks and Lamar phases in

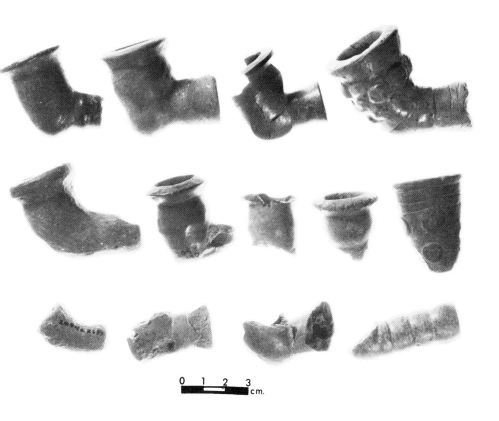

0   1   2   3
cm.

PLATE 46. Selection of clay pipes from the Warren Wilson site (the pipe at the upper left is stone).

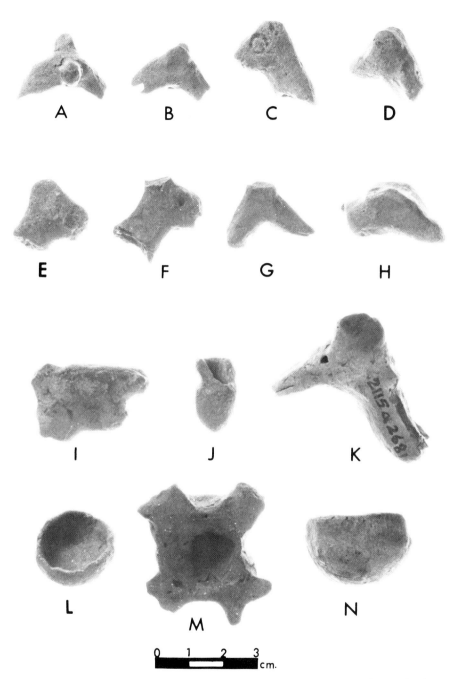

PLATE 47. Clay artifacts from the Warren Wilson site. A-H and K, animal heads; I, bear? effigy; J and L-N, miniature vessels.

PLATE 48. Selection of clay beads from the Warren Wilson site.

northern Georgia, and by Coe (personal communication) for the
Pee Dee phase. Beads from these other cultures lack the variety of
form exhibited by the Pisgah beads.

Several miniature pottery vessels (Plate 47J, L-M) were found at
the Warren Wilson site. These were crude representations of the full-
size Pisgah vessels and probably were made for toys or were chil-
ren's learning efforts.

BONE ARTIFACTS

At the Warren Wilson and Garden Creek sites, bone artifacts were
relatively common in pit fill, where preservation was optimum, but
were generally absent in the overlying plow-disturbed midden. Bone
tools consisted mostly of pointed implements (awls, punches, and
possibly needles) made from larger bone segments or small splinters.
The splinter tools (Plate 49) usually exhibited little use wear, whereas the more carefully manufactured tools of deer ulna and metatarsi
and turkey tarsometatarsi (Plate 50) usually had polished and reworked tips, evidence of more extended use. Several tools with
blunt ends (Plate 50, upper right) may have been used in hide finishing, and several grooved bones and antler tines (Plate 51D-I) may
have served as projectile points. Two bone artifacts resembling awls,
one made from a deer ulna and the other from a turkey tarsometa-
tarsal, were found next to the skull of Burial 7 at the Warren Wilson
site (Plate 52A). Two finely carved bone pins (Plate 51A, B) and a
knobbed antler "ear pin" (Plate 51C) were found in the general
midden at the Warren Wilson site.

Bone tools comparable to the ones recovered in Pisgah contexts
have a broad temporal and spatial distribution in the Southeast. A
comparable assemblage, well described and illustrated, is attributed
to the Dallas component at Hiwassee Island (Lewis and Kneberg
1946:124-126 and Plates 77, 78, 79). Similar carved bone and antler
pins were found in Dallas contexts at Hiwassee Island (Lewis and
Kneberg 1946:125-126 and Plates 78B, 79A) and in "large-log town
house" (Dallas) contexts in the Norris Basin (Webb 1938:Plates 67b,
119b).

The remains of turtle shell rattles were found with Burials 16 and
29 (Plate 53), both adult males, at the Warren Wilson site and with
Burial 18 at Garden Creek Mound No. 1. In all three cases there
were two rattles, one at each ankle. The carapaces of young box

PLATE 49. Selection of bone splinter tools from the Warren Wilson site.

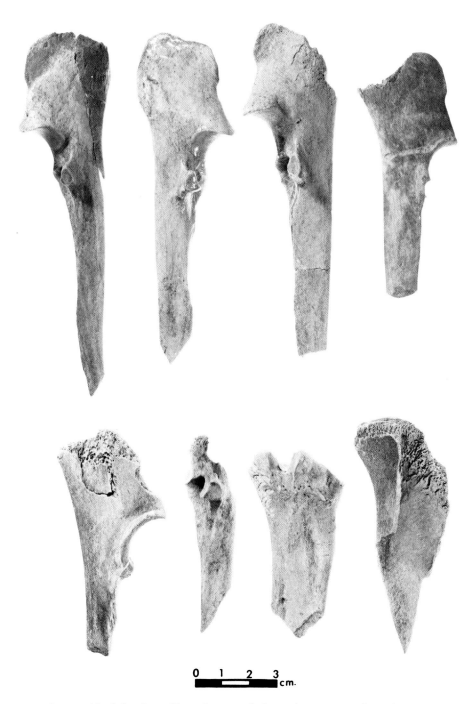

PLATE 50. Selection of large bone tools from the Warren Wilson site.

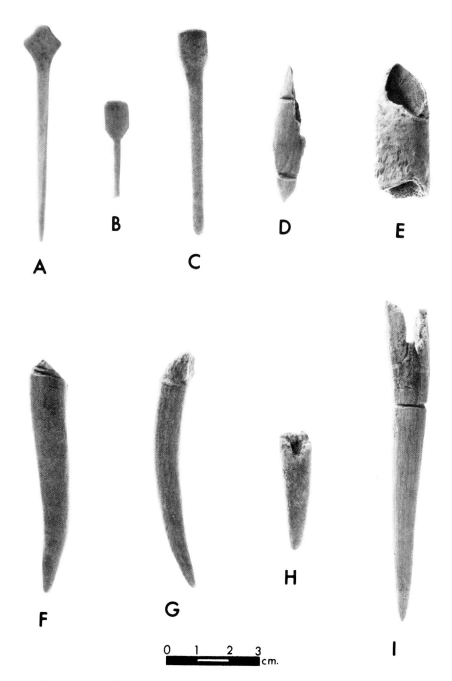

PLATE 51. Bone artifacts from the Warren Wilson site. A and B, carved bone pins; C, antler ear pin; D and E, bone points; F-I, grooved antler tines.

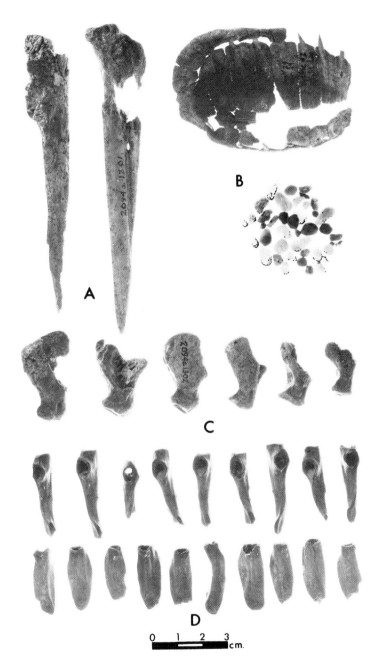

PLATE 52. Bone grave goods from the Warren Wilson site. A, bone awls from Burial 7; B, turtle shell rattle (carapace and pebbles) from Burial 29; C, panther claws from Burial 7; D, perforated rabbit bones from Burial 33.

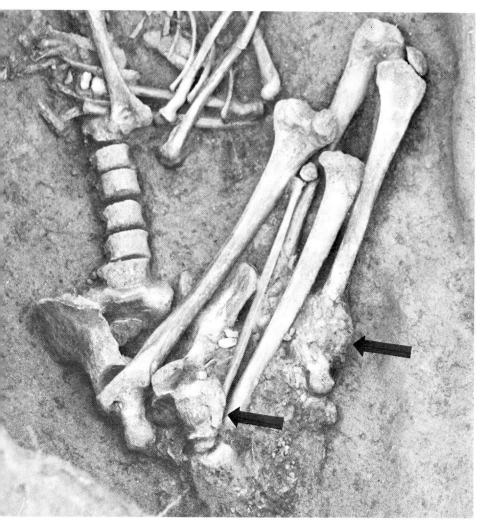

PLATE 53. Close-up of turtle shell rattles at the ankles of Burial 29 at the Warren Wilson site.

turtles *(Terrapene carolina)* had been scraped on the inside and filled with 20 to 30 small (2 to 5 mm) round pebbles. There was a pair of tying holes on one especially well preserved specimen from Burial 29 (Plate 52B). Other turtle shell rattles have been found in Dallas burials at Hiwassee Island (Lewis and Kneberg 1946:126-127), but they were located at the arms rather than the ankles. Caches of small pebbles, possible evidence of rattles for which the casings had decomposed, were found in burials in the Pickwick Basin (Webb and DeJarnette 1942:223 and Plate 254), at the Chauga site, South Carolina (Kelly and Neitzel 1961:29), and at the Town Creek site, North Carolina (Joffre Coe, personal communication).

Thirty-six perforated rabbit *(Sylvilagus sp.)* innominates and scapulae were found in the area of the lower legs of Burial 33 at the Warren Wilson site (Plate 52D). The innominates were perforated through the acetabulum, and the scapulae had the edges of the spinous processes, acromions, and glenoid cavities ground off, and were perforated just above the ventral end. These bones may have been sewn to a garment or strung as anklets. Perforated rabbit pelves have been found at several historic Siouan sites on the Carolina Piedmont (Joffre Coe, personal communication) and in two burials in the McLean Mound near Fayetteville, North Carolina (McCord 1966:27 and Plate 4). Coe (personal communication) suggests a date of A.D. 1350-1450 for the "sand mound complex" to which the McLean site belongs. Six terminal phalanges from a large cat *(Felis concolor)* were found at the left shoulder of Burial 7 at the Warren Wilson site (Plates 52C, 54).

SHELL ARTIFACTS

Evidence for the use of shell for technological purposes was absent at the western North Carolina sites, although a few fragments of freshwater mollusk shell were occasionally found in pit fill along with other food residue. In eastern Tennessee, however, Richard Polhemus (personal communication) reports finding perforated mussel shell "hoes" and Pisgah sherds tempered with crushed shell.

At the Warren Wilson and Garden Creek sites, shell artifacts were made exclusively from marine mollusks, and with the exception of a few small shell beads recovered in pit fill, these artifacts were found only as burial associations. Shell from various-sized, usually adult, conchs *(Busycon sp.)* was the most common raw material.

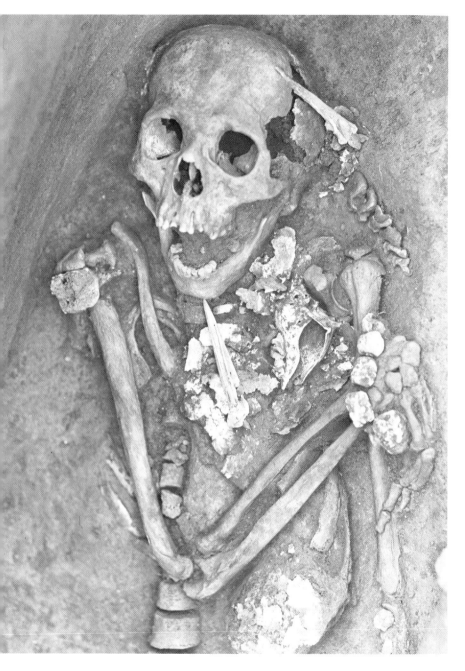

PLATE 54. Close-up of bone awls, columella bead bracelet, small conch shell, mica discs, and panther claws in Burial 7 at the Warren Wilson site.

Large beads (1.5 to 4 cm in diameter) were made from sections of the columella, ground into barrel-shaped or oblong spheroids and drilled lengthwise (Plates 55, 56, 57). Groups of these beads were found as bracelets (Plate 58) or necklaces (Plate 59) in five burials at the Warren Wilson site and in four burials at Garden Creek Mound No. 1. Small disc or cylindrical beads, made from the wall of the conch, were found as necklaces (Plate 56) in eight burials at Garden Creek Mound No. 1, three burials at Garden Creek Mound No. 2, and two burials at the Warren Wilson site. As noted earlier, a few of these small beads were also found as random inclusions in pit fill.

Small and large (columella) conch shell beads have been found with burials of the Dallas phase on the upper Tennessee drainage (Lewis and Kneberg 1946:129 and Plates 82, 84; Webb 1938:Plate 64), the Wilbanks and early Lamar phases in northern Georgia (Wauchope 1966:198, 207, 209; Kelly and Larson 1954:22-27), and the Pee Dee phase on the Carolina Piedmont (Joffre Coe, personal communication), and they have been found in burials of uncertain provenience (probably Savannah phase) at the Irene site (Caldwell and McCann 1941:53-54).

Shell pins fashioned from a section of the conch columella were found in a pair (Plates 57, 58) with Burial 13 at the Warren Wilson site and as a single with Burial 1 at Garden Creek Mound No. 1. These were pointed at one end, had a knob at the other end, and were from 7 to 9 cm long. In both burials, the pins were positioned adjacent to the temporal bones, which suggests a function as ear ornaments. Similar shell pins have been found in Dallas and Mouse Creek phase burials in eastern Tennessee (Lewis and Kneberg 1946: 129-131 and Plates 82, 84; Webb 1938:Plate 64; Kneberg 1952:213 and Figures 109, 110), Wilbanks and Lamar phase burials in northern Georgia (Wauchope 1966:198, 203; Lewis Larson, personal communication), Savannah and Irene phase burials on the Georgia-South Carolina Coastal Plain (Caldwell and McCann 1941:54, 75 and Plate 19), Pee Dee phase burials on the Carolina Piedmont (Joffre Coe, personal communication), and Woodside phase burials at the Slone site in southeastern Kentucky (Dunnell, Hanson, and Hardesty 1971:66 and Figure 40).

Burial 16 at the Warren Wilson site (Plate 59) and Burial 16 at Garden Creek Mound No. 1 each contained a large conch shell bowl. In both cases the interior structure of the shells had been removed and the edges ground. Similar bowls (also called vessels, cups, dip-

PLATE 55. Columella bead bracelets and small conch shell from Burial 7 at the Warren Wilson site.

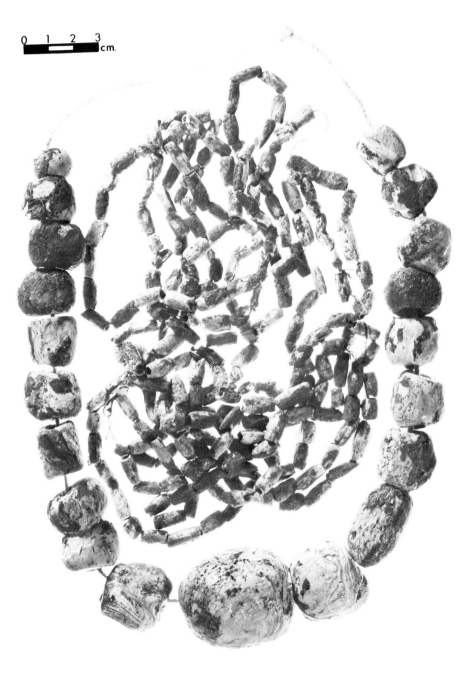

PLATE 56. Columella bead necklace and tubular shell bead necklace from Burial 15 at the Warren Wilson site.

0 1 2 3 cm.

PLATE 57. Columella bead bracelets and columella ear pins from Burial 13 at the Warren Wilson site.

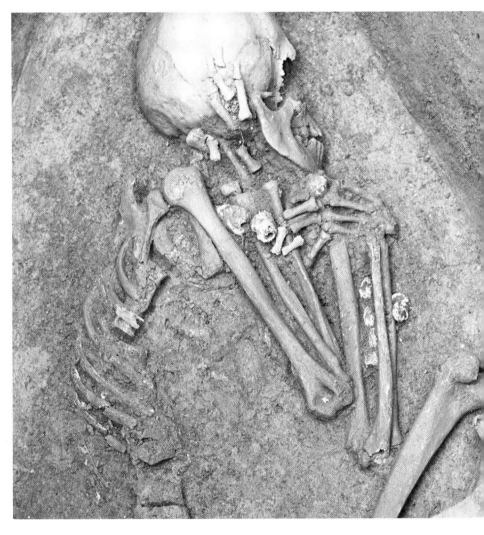

PLATE 58. Close-up of Burial 13 at the Warren Wilson site, showing columella bead bracelets (ear pins are under the right hand, adjacent to each mastoid process).

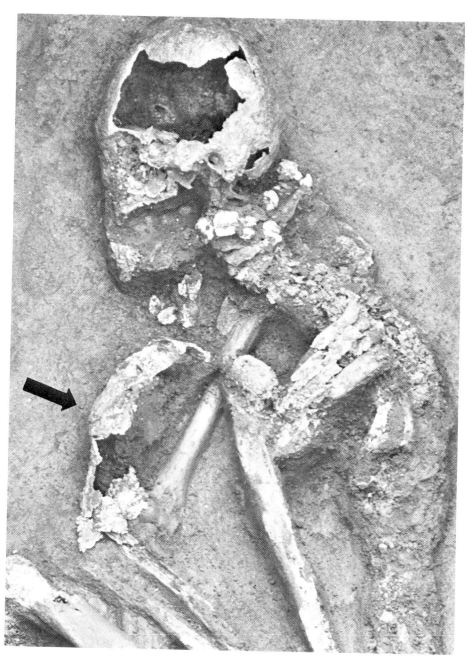

PLATE 59. Close-up of Burial 16 at the Warren Wilson site, showing a columella bead necklace and a large conch shell bowl.

pers, and trumpets) have been reported for the Dallas and Mouse Creek phases (Lewis and Kneberg 1946:130-131; Kneberg 1952: 213-220 and Figure 109); mature Mississippian phases in northern Georgia (Wauchope 1966:209); and the Savannah phase at the Irene site (Caldwell and McCann 1941:54, 75 and Plate 19). A small, unaltered conch shell filled with red ocher was found at the left shoulder of Burial 7 at the Warren Wilson site (Plates 54, 55).

Perforated *Marginella* shells were found with Burials 5 and 26 at the Warren Wilson site and Burial 2 at Garden Creek Mound No. 2. In all three cases these were associated with shell gorgets in the burials of infants. The arrangement of the shells in the pelvic region suggests that they were sewn to garments rather than being strung. *Marginella* beads have been reported for the Dallas phase (Lewis and Kneberg 1946:130), the Savannah phase (Caldwell and McCann 1941: 54), and the Woodside phase (Dunnell, Hanson, and Hardesty 1971:63 and Figure 39).

Shell gorgets accompanied three burials at the Warren Wilson site, six burials at Garden Creek Mound No. 1 (Plate 60), and one burial at Garden Creek Mound No. 2. There was a total of 12 specimens, all made from the walls of large conch shells. Ten were circular (Plate 61A-F), and two were cross-shaped (Plate 61G, H). The circular gorgets, from 3 to 7 cm in diameter, were partly engraved and partly excised to produce the desired motif, which was always on the concave face of the disc. The most common motif was a stylized coiled rattlesnake, which Muller (1966:29) has named the "Lick Creek style" (Plate 61A, B, D-F). There was a single example (from Garden Creek Mound No. 1) of a human figure motif, which Kneberg (1959:15-19) has called the "conventionalized dancer design" (Plate 61C).

Basic to the Lick Creek style were four engraved concentric circles, with the innermost two circles forming the body of the snake. Four equally spaced slots were cut out along the band between the inner two and outer two circles, and on each of the areas remaining between the slots, a small pit was drilled partly through the shell. Within the inner circle, three sections were cut out to produce a stylized head with an open mouth. On the head, which faced to the right on some gorgets and to the left on others, was an incised "forked eye" with a shallow pit to represent the pupil of the eye. The tail of the snake, with rattles, was usually depicted just above the head. Two adjacent holes were drilled completely through the top of the gorget to provide a means for suspension.

PLATE 60. Burial 6 at the Garden Creek site, with shell gorgets.

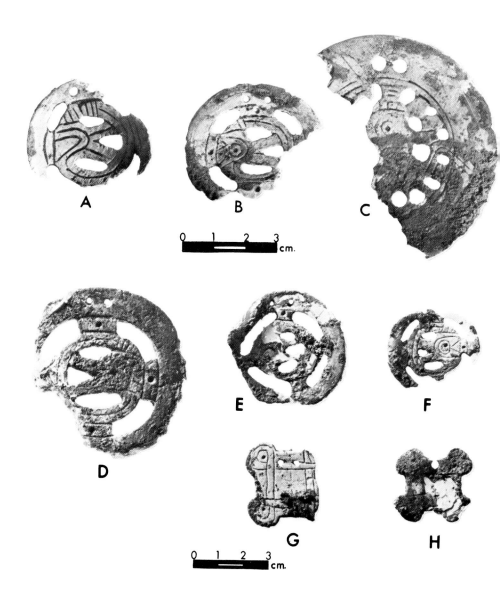

PLATE 61. Shell gorgets. A and B, Lick Creek style gorgets from Garden Creek Mound No. 1; C, stylized human gorget from Garden Creek Mound No. 1; D-F, Lick Creek style gorgets from the Warren Wilson site; G and H, cross-shaped or quadrilobed square gorgets from the Warren Wilson site.

Photographs of the three rattlesnake gorgets from the Warren Wilson site were sent to Jon Muller, who had previously examined similar gorgets from Garden Creek Mound No. 1. His comments on the Lick Creek style and its relationship to the later Citico style are as follows:

> The three rattlesnake theme gorgets from the Warren Wilson site are executed in the style which I have named the Lick Creek style. This style is characteristic of the area north of Knoxville in the Clinch and Holston drainages during the period following the "Southern Cult" proper. The style also extends into the western portion of North Carolina. There is no evidence that any one center in this area was responsible for the manufacture or distribution of these objects. Indeed, there is evidence from several sites of the local nature of the tradition. I would estimate that the Lick Creek style started sometime around the middle of the 15th century or slightly earlier and persisted to the end of the 16th century. At the end of the Lick Creek style, new directions were followed which probably led to the development of a more stylized treatment which I have called the Citico style [see Muller 1966:25-39]. Despite great differences in this general area in ceramic technology, the art in shell in the Lick Creek and Citico styles seems relatively uniform over the area.
>
> In more detailed terms, the three specimens from the Warren Wilson site fall into a hypothetical second phase of the Lick Creek style. One of the characteristics of this phase is the use of a single-line border for the head. These particular specimens, however, are a special kind of Lick Creek gorget which is usually very small in size and is characterized by greatly simplified structures and forms including the "forked eye" treatment on the head. These simplified gorgets seem usually to have been found with infant or child burials. From this view, the simplified treatment is the result of deletions and simplifications of designs found on more complex, larger gorgets rather than an indication of an early place in the development of the style. While the smaller gorgets do not seem to be earlier than the more complex gorgets, it is possible that they are present in all three hypothetical phases of the Lick Creek style and perhaps even in the transitional phases in the development of the Citico style.
>
> One difficulty is that provenience data are so very poor for most of the material from eastern Tennessee. Specimens with details on associations are very rare. Accordingly, a number of alternative explanations of the data are conceivable. One of these is that some of the differences among these "phases" may be reflections of social and regional differences [Jon Muller, personal communication].

Other Lick Creek gorgets have been reported by Muller (1966) for northern Georgia and eastern Tennessee. Examples of the Tennessee specimens are illustrated by Holmes (1884:Figures 121, 124) and by Muller (1966:Figure 2). Some of these have bands of criss-crossed incisions on the body of the snake, representations of the rattles, and additional patterns around the eye and mouth. One of the specimens from Garden Creek Mound No. 1 exhibited some of this elaboration. The eastern Tennessee examples are associated with the Dallas phase (Kneberg 1959:39; Whiteford 1952:220).

The two cross-shaped (or quadrilobed square) gorgets from the Warren Wilson site were found in Burial 5 in association with a slightly larger Lick Creek gorget. One of the specimens was better preserved than the other, and an engraved motif could be delineated. This motif was composed of two parallel lines that followed the outline of the outer edge of the gorget with loops at each corner lobe. At the center of each loop was a shallow drilled pit. On one edge, intersecting the outer line, two suspension holes were drilled completely through the gorget. The second specimen was slightly smaller than the first, and was so heavily encrusted that no engraving could be detected. It had a single suspension hole. Muller's comments on the two cross-shaped gorgets are as follows:

> The other two gorgets from Burial 5 at the Warren Wilson site portray a cross theme that is very difficult to place stylistically. This rather simple theme may well have started in early Mississippian times in the region between Chattanooga and Knoxville [see Kneberg 1959:4-5], but the theme persists until very late times in the same area. To the best of my knowledge, however, these are the only examples of the theme ever recovered together with Lick Creek gorgets. It is probable that these were either brought in from the Tennessee Valley or were copies of items from that area. Contacts between prehistoric Carolina and Tennessee are already attested to by the association at the Canton site [Garden Creek Mound No. 1] of Lick Creek gorgets with a stylized human gorget of very late "Dallas" phase time [Jon Muller, personal communication].

The "stylized human gorget," to which Muller refers, resembles those classified by Kneberg (1959:15-19) as the "conventionalized dancer design," found primarily in Dallas contexts in eastern Tennessee.

WOODEN ARTIFACTS

Evidence for wooden artifacts was present in both direct and indirect forms. Charred split-cane matting was found on a house floor in the village area at the Garden Creek site (Plate 28). Impressions of similar matting were present on the benches of Earth Lodge 2 at Garden Creek, and charred fragments of split cane were recovered in pit fill at the Warren Wilson site. Digging sticks were evidenced by the marks found on pit walls at both sites. Cloth, net, and cord impressions were present on some Pisgah potsherds and occasionally on bits of unfired pottery clay found in pit fill.

TEMPORAL RELATIONSHIPS

On the basis of artifact and ceramic[3] styles and the few available radiocarbon dates, it seems likely that the Pisgah artifact assemblage just described, coming mostly from just two sites, represents a late subphase of the Pisgah development. This subphase, with a suggested dating of A.D. 1250-1450, is removed by about four centuries from the late Connestee phase, and this difference in time limits my comparisons of the Pisgah and Connestee artifact assemblages.

Keel has defined in detail the Connestee artifact assemblage at four sites in western North Carolina, and he has made some specific comparisons of this assemblage with the remains from several sites in Tennessee and Georgia (Keel 1972: Keel and Chapman n.d.). He assigns the Connestee phase a temporal placement of ca. A.D. 300-1000 (Keel 1972:286). When we compare this Connestee assemblage with the late Pisgah assemblage, we find that the closest correspondences are for artifacts having primarily technological function. For example, there are similarities in the pecked stone tools and bone tools, and the several types of small to medium-sized triangular projectile points identified with the Connestee phase (Keel 1972:173-179) could easily represent ancestral forms of the small triangular points of the Pisgah phase.

Artifacts with greater propensity for stylistic variation, such as ceramics (discussed in detail in the following chapter), have fewer correspondences, and in artifacts of presumed sociological and ideological importance, such as ornamentation and grave furniture (although few specifically identifiable Connestee burials have been reported for the North Carolina sites), there are no recognizable relationships. The Connestee artifacts of Hopewellian relationship, or even any descendent forms of such artifacts, are totally lacking in the Pisgah assemblage.

3. Evidence for two stylistic subphases of Pisgah pottery is presented in Ch. 5.

Thus, in the total artifact assemblages, and especially in the categories that presumably would be more indicative of social and ideological trends, there appears to have been a major break between Connestee and Pisgah. However, no early Pisgah sites have been investigated, and an assemblage that is intermediate between Connestee and Pisgah may even be discovered.

In the artifact assemblage of the Qualla phase,[4] technological items, including all of the pecked stone categories, ground stone celts and discs, chipped stone points and flake tools, and bone tools, are nearly identical in form, materials, and technique of manufacture to corresponding objects in the late Pisgah assemblage. There are obvious developmental connections in ceramics (see Chapter 5) and in other clay artifacts, such as pipes, discs, and beads. A few new forms were added, such as clay pipes with zoomorphic, "monolithic axe," "trumpet," and other embellished bowl designs (Setzler and Jennings 1941:Plate 20). Shell grave furniture, such as beads, ear pins, and gorgets, show considerable continuity in form and decorative style from late Pisgah to early Qualla. For example, the obviously related Lick Creek and Citico gorget styles may have been, as Muller (1966:37) suggests, "the different styles of the same society or societies at different points in time."

Finally, there is considerable evidence that certain artifact types of the Pisgah phase, e.g., rectangular celts, stone discs, elbow pipes, cut mica discs, turtle shell rattles, and shell gorgets with a rattlesnake design, have a specific distribution in South Appalachian cultures of the late prehistoric period. This distribution focuses on the western North Carolina, eastern Tennessee, and Georgia-South Carolina Piedmont areas and is roughly coterminous with the boundaries of Cherokee occupations in the early historic period. In the Appalachian Summit itself, significant overlaps occur between artifact styles of the Pisgah phase and those of the succeeding Qualla phase, and numerous Qualla sites have been positively identified (Egloff 1967) with the protohistoric and historic Cherokees.

---

4. There are, as yet, few published descriptions of Qualla artifacts. The Peachtree Mound report (Setzler and Jennings 1941:Plates 10-30, excepting a few obvious Archaic and Woodland specimens) has the most completely illustrated sample. I have examined materials from a number of surface collections, as well as from excavations at the Coweeta Creek site (Figure 1) and from various excavations of the Valentine Museum, all of which are housed at the Research Laboratories of Anthropology in Chapel Hill.

5. Ceramics

Archaeologists have long considered pottery styles to be valuable cultural markers. At the same time, they have acknowledged that temporal and spatial distinctions in ceramics may not necessarily indicate ethnic or sociopolitical distinctions. However, if ceramics can be considered broadly to reflect behavioral relationships, then a study of the ceramics of the Pisgah phase will be important in the ultimate interpretation of the origins and evolution of Cherokee culture.

In this chapter, an effort is made to provide detailed and comprehensive descriptions of Pisgah ceramics, to summarize current knowledge of the areal and temporal distributions of these ceramics, to point out possible connections with other South Appalachian pottery, and finally to propose an interpretation of the relationships of Pisgah ceramics to the ceramics of the historic Cherokees.

THE PISGAH SERIES

In 1881, Edward Palmer, working for the Bureau of Ethnology, excavated a mound on the French Broad River near Newport, Tennessee (Figure 1). William H. Holmes described the pottery from this site, and his listing included such characteristic Pisgah traits as thickened and collared rims, impressed "herringbone" patterns on the outer surface of the rims, decorated loop handles, and rectilinear complicated stamping, which he described as "groups of parallel indented lines, arranged at right angles with one another" (Holmes 1884:440-441).

Pisgah sherds found in 1958 at the Chauga site (Figure 1), Oconee County, South Carolina, were tentatively assigned the name "pseudo-Iroquois," since the archaeologists felt that the sherds manifest an "attenuated resemblance to prehistoric Iroquoian pottery in the northeastern United States" (Kelly and Neitzel 1961:36-37).

Using sherd collections from Transylvania County, North Carolina, Patricia Holden compiled the first typology for Pisgah ceramics in 1966. Under her Pisgah series, she listed Pisgah Complicated Stamped, Pisgah Smoothed-Over Complicated Stamped, Pisgah Check Stamped, and Pisgah Plain (Holden 1966:72-77). Brian Egloff adopted Holden's types in his 1967 study of ceramics from selected historic Cherokee towns (Egloff 1967).

Also in 1966, Richard and James Polhemus published a description of Pisgah sherds from sites on the Clinch and Holston rivers in Tennessee under the name Cobb Island Complicated Stamped. Although they did not assign additional type names, they listed four other forms of surface finish for this pottery: check stamping, linear check stamping, herringbone stamping, and diamond stamping within a "stair step pattern" (Polhemus and Polhemus 1966:13-24).

C. G. Holland's Lee series pottery of southwestern Virginia also conforms in most respects to the descriptions that are to follow for the Pisgah series. Holland recognized four types: Lee Linear Stamped, Lee Check Stamped, Lee Plain, and Lee Simple Stamped (Holland 1970:58-61).

In compiling the present descriptions, I utilized surface-collected and excavated sherds from sites in western North Carolina, northeastern Tennessee, northwestern South Carolina, and southwestern Virginia.[1] Included were 30,144 sherds from excavations at the Warren Wilson site (a sample of 4,125 sherds from feature and burial pit fill is listed in Table 5).

TYPE DESCRIPTIONS[2]

PISGAH RECTILINEAR COMPLICATED STAMPED

Paste:

Method of Manufacture:
Thin annular strips were coiled around a basal plate. Coils usually were well eradicated in the finished vessel.

1. I am grateful to Richard and James Polhemus for permission to examine and photograph sherds in their collections from the Clinch and Holston rivers in Tennessee; and to Wesley Breedlove for making available his well-documented collections from the upper Saluda River in South Carolina. Dr. C. G. Holland kindly supplied me with a typewritten copy of his manuscript, "An Archaeological Survey of Southwest Virginia," which included descriptions of his Lee series pottery and photographs of some of the type sherds.
2. These type descriptions follow the format of the Ceramic Repository of the Museum of Anthropology at the University of Michigan (see Sears and Griffin 1950).

Table 5. Pisgah Ceramic Types from Feature and Burial Pitfill at the Warren Wilson Site.

	Rect. Comp. A	Rect. Comp. B	Rect. Comp. C	Curv. Comp.	Check	Plain Smooth	Plain Rough	Cord Mkd.	Uniden.	Total
Feature										
2	15						1		18	34
3	1								6	7
4	5	1	1	1	1				10	19
5	1						1		4	6
6	1						1		2	4
7	395	96	30	8	59	13	10	1	478	1090
8	3								5	8
9	3				1				4	8
14					3				6	9
37	15								11	26
40	2	3			1				5	11
41	5								7	12
47	36	5							35	76
53	16	2			1				23	42
54	12	3			6				27	48
55	8								4	12
56	29	15	2	1	5	3			28	83
57	280			9	11		6		545	851
85	23								15	38
86	73				4	4	4		25	110
107	27	3			15	4			38	87
108	55	4		2	6	4	1		32	104
136	198	88		1	17	2	1		152	459
137	22	4			2				24	52
140	62				6	9			21	98
Burial										
1	6								2	8
2	2								3	5
3	2									2
4										0
5	3								5	8
6									1	1
7	33				1	1	1		47	83
8	23	1			1	3	1		12	41
9										0
10	5				1				1	7
11	7									7
12	14				1				9	24
13	36	4				2	5		38	85
14	1				1	1			4	7
15	26	4		1	2		1		34	68
16	9				2				21	32
17	8				4				19	31
18	25			7	9	1			24	66
19	45				5				20	70
20	8								8	16
21	41	1			7	1			48	98
22	14	2							24	40
23	7	4			2	1			21	35
24	1	2							1	4
25	2				1					3
26	8								12	20
27	4	2			1				6	13
28	9			1	1				13	24
29	1				1				2	4
30	2								2	4
31										0
32	1	1							3	5
33	3	2			3		1		11	20
TOTALS	1633	247	33	31	181	49	34	1	1916	4125

Temper:
Fine to coarse sand, with particles usually about 0.1-0.5 mm. Scattered inclusions may be as large as 3 mm. Fine mica flecks are abundant, particularly in sherds from western North Carolina. Crushed-quartz temper, found occasionally, is probably early. A few shell tempered sherds are present in collections from Tennessee, and some steatite tempered sherds are found in northwestern North Carolina and extreme northeastern Tennessee; both are probably late in the Pisgah development.

Texture:
Usually fairly even and compact. Temper particles comprise from 20 to 40 percent of the paste.

Hardness:
2 to 3; varies with intensity of firing, abundance of temper particles, and degree of weathering.

Color:
Interior surfaces are gray to almost black; exterior surfaces are usually light gray, tan, or buff. Sometimes several colors are found on the same sherd.

Surface Finish (exterior):

Rectilinear complicated stamping is present on about 80 to 90 percent of the sherds in collections from western North Carolina. This percentage is higher in some Tennessee collections and lower in some South Carolina collections. Three slightly different rectilinear designs (designated A, B, and C) have been identified thus far, all of which appear to have been applied with a carved wooden paddle.

Rectilinear Design A:
This design is the most common form of surface finish, about 75 percent in western North Carolina collections (Figure 17 and Plate 62A-D). The basic motif is formed by two (or sometimes three or four) vertical lines flanked by rows of eight or more horizontal lines. The horizontal lines are usually shorter and slightly more closely spaced than the vertical lines. The potter began the stamping at the base of the vessel, and after completing one circuit, continued with a new row directly above the first. It appears that an effort usually was made to stagger the design from row to row, creating an uneven line-block effect. Often, the impressions on one row overlapped slightly those of the preceding row, partially eradicating the earlier impressions. In some cases, the intersecting rows were not kept parallel, causing portions of adjacent impressions to crisscross.

Two varieties of Design A have been recognized. In one, the horizontal elements are short (10 mm or less), and the lands and grooves are relatively narrow, usually about 0.75-1.5 mm (Figure 17 and Plate 62D, G).

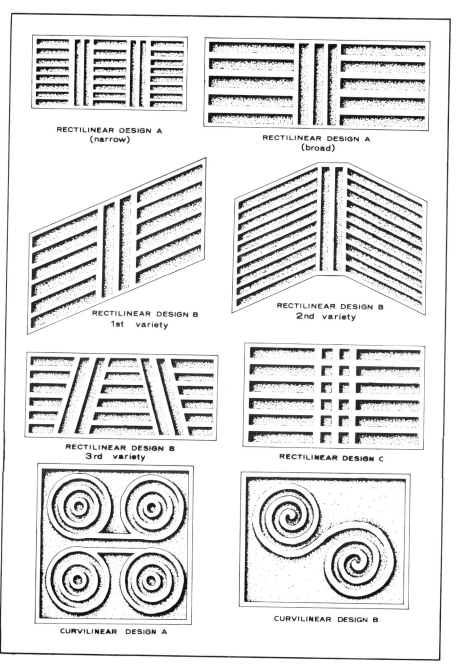

RECTILINEAR DESIGN A
(narrow)

RECTILINEAR DESIGN A
(broad)

RECTILINEAR DESIGN B
1st variety

RECTILINEAR DESIGN B
2nd variety

RECTILINEAR DESIGN B
3rd variety

RECTILINEAR DESIGN C

CURVILINEAR DESIGN A

CURVILINEAR DESIGN B

FIGURE 17. Pisgah Complicated Stamped designs.

PLATE 62. Pisgah sherds. A-D, Pisgah Rectilinear Complicated Stamped, Design A (A-C, broad variety; D, narrow variety); E-H, Pisgah Rectilinear Complicated Stamped, Design B (E, first variety; F, second variety; G and H, third variety); I, Pisgah Rectilinear Complicated Stamped, Design C.

In the other variety, the horizontal elements are long (20 to 40 mm), and the individual lands and grooves are broad (1-4 mm) (Figure 17; Plate 62A-C). Present evidence indicates that the small variety of Design A began earlier in time than the bold variety, and that it probably evolved out of small rectilinear designs occasionally found on earlier Connestee pottery. The bold variety seems to be later in time. In most of western North Carolina, the small variety is found less commonly than the bold variety, and is usually present on small jars with unmodified or thickened rims. In Tennessee and parts of northwestern South Carolina, the small variety is in the majority; here it is present on small to medium-sized jars with rims that are unmodified or thickened or have short, thick collars. The bold variety is found most abundantly on sites in the upper French Broad and Pigeon basins of western North Carolina. It is almost always present on relatively large, collared jars, or on small bowls with straight rims or inslanted rims.

Rectilinear Design B:
This design differs from Design A in that either the vertical or the horizontal grooves are slanted. Three varieties have been identified. In one, the alternating sets of vertical grooves are parallel, with the flanking grooves slanted in the same direction (Figure 17; Plate 62E). In a second variety, the flanking grooves alternate in direction, one set running up and the next down (Figure 17; Plate 62F). In a third variety, the vertical grooves are alternately slanted to form open-ended "V's" (Figure 17; Plate 62G, H). In all three varieties of Design B the execution is usually bold (Plate 62E, F, H), although small examples do occur (Plate 62G), and they usually are found on large vessels. Design B is most prevalent in western North Carolina collections, occurring on about 10 percent of the sherds. It is found infrequently in Tennessee and South Carolina. Polhemus and Polhemus (1966:17-18) probably are referring to the second-described variety of this design when they speak of a "herring-bone stamp."

Rectilinear Design C:
This design differs from Design A in that instead of the central grooves being continuous, they are broken to form checks or small rectangles (Figure 17; Plate 62I). The execution is always rather bold, and it probably is a late form. This design was not observed outside of western North Carolina, where it was present on about 1 percent of the sherds.

Surface Finish (Interior):
The interior surface finish ranges from lightly smoothed to burnished. In most cases, there was enough smoothing to float the finer clay particles and mica flecks to the surface. Infrequently, the interior surface is rough.

Decoration:

The most striking feature of Pisgah pottery is the varied and sometimes ornate decoration of the rim area. Since the form of the rim appears to have had a great deal to do with determining its decoration, descriptions of decorative styles are taken up under three categories of rim form—collared, thickened, and unmodified.

Collared rims:

The most common decoration on collared rims is a series of short diagonal punctations (Plate 63I-K, M, N). The individual impressions range from narrow slits to bold gashes. These are commonly in two or three parallel rows, although there may be only a single row or as many as four rows. The impressions usually are arranged diagonally to the rim, with the direction alternating on each row; a double row forming open-ended chevrons is typical (Plate 62F). Sometimes the collar is decorated with one or two horizonal incised lines (Plate 62D) or with combinations of incisions and punctations (Plate 62C). Oblique-angled incised patterns (Plate 63P) are occasionally present on sherds from western North Carolina and northwestern South Carolina. In rare instances collars are undecorated (Plate 63O), and on a few sherds they are stamped with the same design as the body of the vessel (Plate 63L).

Thickened rims:

A thickened rim may be decorated along the top of the lip with patterns similar to those used on collared rims, but since the area is more restricted, this decoration usually consists of only one or two rows of punctations or a single incised line (Plate 63C-H). Occasionally there is no decration, or the decoration may be just below the lip.

Unmodified rims:

Unmodified (i.e., uncollared or unthickened) rims are decorated about 50 percent of the time. A straight form is occasionally punctated in similar fashion to the collared rim (Plate 63Q), or more frequently there is an appliqued strip with closely spaced pinches or notches along the top-outside of the lip (Plate 63R). An everted form usually is undecorated, but occasionally it has punctations similar to those on collared rims. An inslanted form may be undecorated, punctated, or incised with oblique-angled patterns, similar to Dallas Incised (Plate 63S).

Form:

Rim:

In western North Carolina, about 80 percent of the rims are everted, 15 percent are straight, and 5 percent are inslanted (Figure 18). The inslanted form is less abundant in South Carolina and Tennessee collections. There are also fewer straight rims in Tennessee collections.

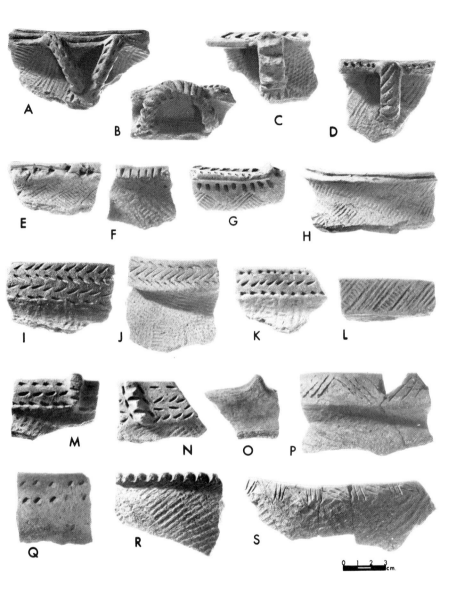

PLATE 63. Pisgah rim sherds. A-D, thickened rims with appendages; E-H, thickened rims with various decorations; I-K, collared rims with punctations; L, collared rim with rectilinear complicated stamping; M and N, collared rims with lugs; O, collared rim undecorated with castellation; P, collared rim with incised decoration; Q, straight rim with punctations; R, straight rim with notched strip; S, inslanted rim with incised decoration.

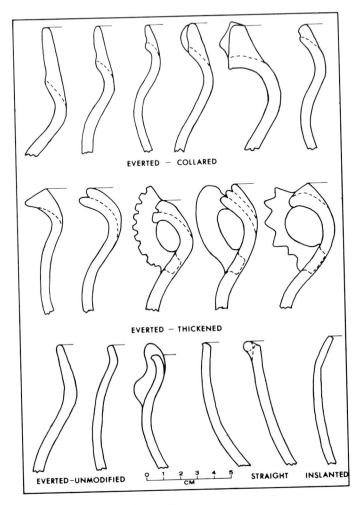

EVERTED — COLLARED

EVERTED — THICKENED

EVERTED-UNMODIFIED   STRAIGHT   INSLANTED

0 1 2 3 4 5
CM

FIGURE 18. Pisgah rim profiles.

The everted rim usually has a collar, which was constructed by the addition of a strip of clay around the top interior of the lip. These collars are approximately the same thickness as the rest of the vessel and 7-40 mm high (tall collars are usually found on larger vessels). In most cases the outer face of the collar was carefully aligned with the original lip, and the inner face was smoothed to erase its juncture with the interior surface of the vessel. In some cases, the collar was set back slightly, leaving the original lip protruding. If the rim was sharply everted, the area behind the collar might be filled with additional clay to even out the interior vessel wall; these greatly everted, thick-collared rims are abundant in Tennessee collections. Collared rims were present early in the Pisgah development and seem to have persisted longer than the thickened form. After their appearance, collars gradually became taller through time as vessels became larger; however, some small vessels with short collars were made even at a very late date. Everted rims were sometimes thickened without the addition of a collar. This was done by molding one or two strips of clay to the interior of the rim. The top of the thickening either was flattened or was left with the unaltered ridges. Thickened, everted rims seem to have been early in time, since the accompanying stamps are almost always either the narrow variety of Design A or small checks. Everted rims without thickening or collars were present throughout the sequence but probably were most numerous in the early phase.

Straight rims usually are unmodified, but they sometimes are thickened in the manner described above (an early form) or have a thin pinched or notched strip around the top exterior of the lip (a late form).

Some rims are inslanted at an angle of 5° to 30° from the wall of the vessel, with the inslanted portion measuring 15-25 mm. This form of rim probably was introduced to the Pisgah area from the Ridge and Valley or Piedmont region after about A.D. 1250.

Lip:
Either rounded, flattened, or ridged.

Body:
Globular jars and open bowls (Figure 19). Orifice diameters are 10-40 cm. The average vessel size is larger for the late phase.

Base:
Rounded to slightly pointed on jars; rounded to slightly flattened on bowls.

Thickness:
Vessel walls are 4.5-8.5 mm thick (6.5 mm average for western North Carolina sherds). Basal and rim sherds may be somewhat thicker.

Appendages:
The rims of Pisgah vessels may be decorated with any one, or a combina-

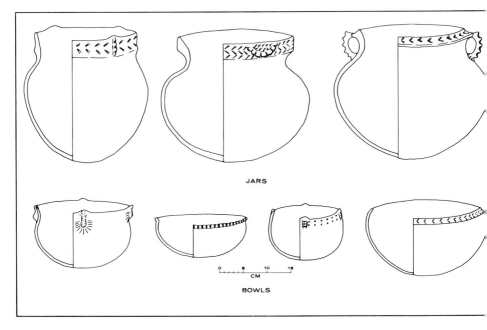

JARS

BOWLS

FIGURE 19. Pisgah vessel forms.

tion, of several appendages. Appliqued strips (attached either horizontally or in "U" or "V" fashion), vertical lugs, nodes, and small castellations (frequently in combination with nodes or lugs) are found on collared rims (Plates 62C; 63B, G, M-O). Loop handles (usually themselves notched, incised, or punctated) are common on thickened rims but rare on collared rims (Plates 62D; 63A, C, D). There are rare examples of strap handles on late Pisgah vessels (Plate 65F).

PISGAH CURVILINEAR COMPLICATED STAMPED

Paste:

The same as Pisgah Rectilinear Complicated Stamped, but no crushed quartz or shell temper was observed.

Surface Finish:

Curvilinear stamped designs are present on about 1 to 2 percent of Pisgah sherds from sites in western North Carolina, where the major occupations are presumed to have been in the late phase. They were not observed by Holden (1966) in the Transylvania County, North Carolina, collections, nor were any reported by Polhemus and Polhemus (1966) from the Clinch and Holston rivers in Tennessee. Curvilinear stamping probably can be attributed to southerly influences, first from Savannah/Wilbanks and Pee Dee, and later from Lamar. Curvilinear motifs are prevalent in the later Qualla Complicated Stamped (Egloff 1967). The exterior surface exhibits a complete covering of contiguous curvilinear impressions, applied with a carved wooden paddle. Two distinct designs have been recognized, and are referred to as Designs A and B. The interior surface finish for this type is the same as for Pisgah Rectilinear Complicated Stamped.

Curvilinear Design A:
This design consists of a pair of concentric circles separated from an identical adjacent pair by a single groove (Plate 64B). The outer rings of the circles are 25-35 mm in diameter.

Curvilinear Design B:
This design, found only on a few sherds from western North Carolina, consists of concentric circles in a scroll-like pattern (Plate 64A).

Decoration:

The small number of rim sherds recovered thus far has punctat-

PLATE 64. Pisgah and proto-Pisgah sherds. A, Pisgah Curvilinear Complicated Stamped, Design B; B, Pisgah Curvilinear Complicated Stamped, Design A; C-E, Pisgah Check Stamped; F-J, Connestee Complicated Stamped with proto-Pisgah motifs.

ed collars or pinched, straight rims. No thickened rims or rims with handles have been observed with curvilinear stamping.

Form:

The same as Pisgah Rectilinear Complicated Stamped.

PISGAH CHECK STAMPED

Paste:

The same as Pisgah Rectilinear Complicated Stamped.

Surface Finish:

The entire outer vessel surface is covered with a check design, applied with a carved wooden paddle (Plates 63C, 64C-E). This form of surface finish was present on about 8 to 10 percent of the Pisgah sherds from western North Carolina. Roughly equivalent percentages were noted in collections from South Carolina and Tennessee.

The individual elements of the check pattern are usually square, although a slightly rectangular shape is not infrequent. Only rarely are the elements diamond-shaped. The grooves measure from 2 to 5 mm and the lands from 0.75 to 2 mm; there are from 3 to 8 checks per inch. Small checks seem to be early in time, whereas larger checks probably developed along with bolder rectilinear stamping. Interior surface finishes are the same as Pisgah Rectilinear Complicated Stamped.

Decoration:

The same as Pisgah Rectilinear Complicated Stamped.

Form:

The same as Pisgah Rectilinear Complicated Stamped. Vessels with small checks usually have thickened rims; vessels with large checks usually have collared or unmodified rims.

PISGAH PLAIN

Paste:

The same as Pisgah Rectilinear Complicated Stamped.

Surface Finish:

A plain exterior surface finish was present on 1 to 3 percent of the Pisgah sherds from western North Carolina sites (Plate 63O-Q). The percentage was considerably higher at certain sites on the Keowee River in northwestern South Carolina (Roger Grange, personal communication). There are both smooth and rough varieties. The smooth variety ranges from lightly smoothed to burnished.

Decoration:

The same as Pisgah Rectilinear Complicated Stamped.

Form:

The same as Pisgah Rectilinear Complicated Stamped.

MINORITY SURFACE FINISHES

Pisgah sherds occasionally have surface finishes other than the ones described above (mainly observed in late contexts in western North Carolina). These are as follows: woven-reed (or woven-quill) impressed, cord marked (Plate 65F), and net impressed (Plate 65G). Simple stamping, noted in Tennessee by Polhemus and Polhemus (1966) and in Virginia by Holland (1970), was not encountered by this writer in any of the collections examined.

GEOGRAPHICAL RANGE

Surface-collected sherds were available for a large number of western North Carolina sites, most of which had been located by the Research Laboratories of Anthropology survey teams.[3] Sections of northwestern South Carolina had received good survey coverage through the work of Research Laboratories teams and the efforts of Wesley Breedlove of Marietta. In eastern Tennessee, Research Laboratories teams had made cursory explorations along the lower portions of the Pigeon, French Broad, and Nolichucky rivers; and collections were available from sites on the Clinch and Holston rivers, courtesy of Richard and James Polhemus of Mascot. A few sites

---

3. Haywood County collections were tabulated by Joffre Coe and Bennie Keel, and Transylvania County collections by Patricia Holden (1966:Table 1). I tabulated the remainder.

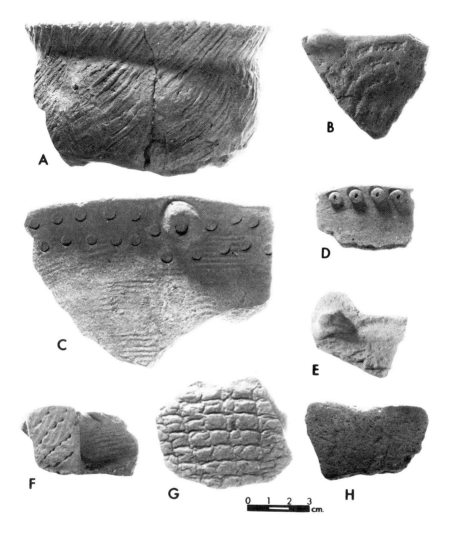

PLATE 65. Unusual sherds from the Warren Wilson site. A, Pisgah Rectilinear Complicated Stamped with Dan River type rim; B, Pisgah Curvilinear Complicated Stamped with Savannah/Wilbanks type motif; C, Pee Dee Complicated Stamped; D, plain with Pee Dee type rim; E, complicated stamped with Dallas type rim; F, cord marked with strap handle; G, net impressed; H, plain with steatite temper.

were reported for southwestern Virginia by C. G. Holland, who kindly provided sherd counts.

In the examination of a surface collection, the first step was to tabulate the total number of sherds, and then to separate out any Pisgah series sherds and record their number and percentage. Finally, the location of the site was recorded on a map of the Southern Appalachian region. On this map a distinction was made between sites where Pisgah sherds amounted to 25 percent or more of the total sherd count and sites where they amounted to less than 25 percent. A distinction at the 25 percent level was not totally arbitrary, as this seemed to represent the level at which a site could be judged clearly to have had a long-term Pisgah occupation as opposed to a site where there had been only a sporadic or brief occupation or possibly only peripheral contact.

I am cognizant of the sampling problems that arise when dealing with surface collections, especially when the collections are obtained by different people and at different times. I am also aware of the wide range of physical and cultural factors that can affect the apportionment of ceramics on a given site. However, since the entire area under consideration is thought to have had an approximately equivalent duration of occupation by ceramic-bearing cultures, and since most of the collections are believed to have been obtained by comparable procedures, the percentages should reflect the relative intensity of distribution of Pisgah ceramics over the Southern Appalachian region (Figure 20). There were weak areas, and even large gaps, in the survey coverage, and the most important of these will be delineated in the following discussions.

NORTH CAROLINA

Survey data are lacking for much of the area along the eastern periphery of the Blue Ridge. Nevertheless, Pisgah sherds were recorded for twelve sites on the upper Catawba River in McDowell County and for seven sites on the upper tributaries of the Nolichucky River in Mitchell and Yancy counties. Sites farther to the east in Burke County contained no Pisgah sherds, but there was an abundance of a related ware called the Burke series (Keeler 1971: Table 8). Burke pottery may be antecedent to the ceramics of the protohistoric Catawba Indians (Joffre Coe, personal communication).

One hundred seven sites, many with high percentages of Pisgah sherds, were recorded on the upper French Broad drainage in Tran-

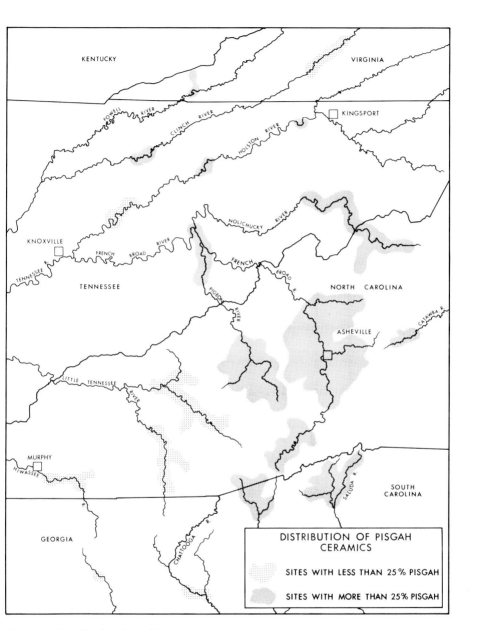

FIGURE 20. Distribution of Pisgah ceramics.

sylvania, Henderson, Buncombe, and Madison counties. Although the Pisgah series is strongly represented in this area, sherds of the subsequent Qualla series are present on only a few sites.

On the upper Pigeon River, in Haywood County, 75 sites with Pisgah ceramics were recorded. This area has the densest concentration of Pisgah sites in the entire Blue Ridge region, possibly a reflection more of intensive survey coverage than of actual distribution. Some sites in this area, such as those on Garden Creek near Canton, have sherds of a late (early 15th century) style of Pisgah which seem to be transitional to Qualla styles (Plate 64E).

For all of far-western North Carolina, along the upper drainages of the Little Tennessee, Tuckasegee, Valley, and Hiwassee rivers, only 32 collections were found to contain Pisgah pottery, and in most of these it was represented by small percentages. As one moves west from the Tuckasegee valley, Pisgah sherds decrease in frequency, but there remains a strong representation of the later Qualla series. A few Pisgah sherds from the Peachtree site, on the Hiwassee River near Murphy, represent the westernmost finds (Setzler and Jennings 1941:Plate 37, A, bottom row, 2 and 4, and Plate 43, middle row, 3 and 5).

In summary, 233 sites containing Pisgah series pottery have been recorded to date in western North Carolina. Although some areas, especially along the eastern fringe of the mountains, are lacking adequate survey data, present evidence indicates that sites with Pisgah ceramics are most abundant on the upper Pigeon and French Broad drainages. The areal distributions of Pisgah and the later Qualla series overlap, but there is a definite shift to the southwest for the latter; sites in the Pigeon and Tuckasegee river areas have the greatest admixture of the two series.

SOUTH CAROLINA AND GEORGIA

In South Carolina, sites with Pisgah sherds were most numerous on the upper drainage of the Saluda River, and there were a few sites farther to the west on the Keowee River and Eastatoe Creek, including two historically documented villages—Toxaway and Eastatoe. The I. C. Few site, on the Keowee River near the site of Fort Prince George, contained a ceramic assemblage which appears to be predominantly Pisgah. Here, surface finishes were mostly plain and check stamped, with only a few sherds being complicated stamped

(Roger Grange, personal communication). Still farther to the west on the Chattooga River, one site with Pisgah sherds has been recorded.

Extensive excavations at the Chauga Mound and village site, located at the juncture of the Tugaloo and Chauga rivers in Oconee County, South Carolina, produced a small amount of Pisgah pottery (Kelly and Neitzel 1961). These sherds, referred to by the excavators as "Pseudo-Iroquoian Punctate" (Kelly and Neitzel 1961:36-37, Plate 11, and illustration VI, lower), made up as much as 5 percent of the pottery in several of the mound stages and in the premound village midden, but it would appear that only rim sherds were identified. J. R. Caldwell (personal communication) also found Pisgah sherds in mound and village middens at the Tugalo site, located on the Georgia side of the Tugaloo River a few miles west of the Chauga site.

TENNESSEE AND VIRGINIA

Only limited surveys have been carried out on the lower courses of the Pigeon, French Broad, and Nolichucky rivers in Tennessee, and it is probable that the few Pisgah sites recorded on these drainages represent only a fraction of the number that would be found through more extensive reconnaissance.

Richard and James Polhemus have recorded nine Pisgah sites on the Clinch and Holston rivers in Grainger, Jefferson, and Claiborne counties, Tennessee, and they suspect the existence of other sites that would presently be covered by the waters of Norris and Cherokee lakes. No Pisgah ceramics have been found by them below the junction of the Holston and French Broad rivers (Richard Polhemus, personal communication). At the Holliston Mills site on the Holston River below Kingsport, Tennessee, the ceramic assemblage is composed of about 70 percent Dallas series sherds and 30 percent Pisgah (Charles Faulkner, personal communication).

A few Pisgah sherds were found at the Rankin site, a primarily Early Woodland site, located on the west bank of the French Broad River at its juncture with the Nolichucky River (Smith and Hodges 1968:84-87). This site also contained an intrusive burial of a young child accompanied by an intact Pisgah vessel (Smith and Hodges 1968:Plate XLIV). The pot was inverted next to the skull (David Smith, personal communication). A mound located at the junction of the French Broad and Pigeon rivers, near Newport, Tennessee, contained pottery that is unquestionably Pisgah (see reference to Holmes at the beginning of this chapter). The northernmost extension of Pisgah ceramics thus far reported is in southwestern Virginia, along the major streams that form the headwaters of the Tennessee River. C. G. Holland (1970) recorded four sites on the Clinch River in Scott County and two sites on the Powell River in Lee County. At both of the Lee County sites and at one of the Scott County sites, Pisgah sherds amounted to more than 25 percent of the total sherd collections.

SITES OUTSIDE THE APPALACHIAN SUMMIT WITH PISGAH CERAMICS

Several Pisgah-like rim sherds were reported by James Reid (1967:62 and Plate VIII, first row) for the Town Creek mound, Montgomery County, North Carolina. Excavations at the Nacoochee Mound on the Upper Chattahoochee River in White County, Georgia, produced a few rim sherds similar to Pisgah forms (Heye, Hodge, and Pepper 1918:Figures 24, 25). And 22 sherds from a single Pisgah Complicated Stamped vessel were found as far afield as the Angel site in southern Indiana (Kellar 1967:480, 484 and Figure 192).

DISTRIBUTION OF PISGAH CERAMICS AT THE WARREN WILSON SITE

Table 6 contains percentage distributions by provenience of Pisgah ceramic types at the Warren Wilson site. Tabulations were compiled for sherds from a random plow zone sample of fifty 10-foot squares and for sherds from all feature and burial fills. Against these two comprehensive populations, comparisons were made of the distributions of the same types in the specific areas of six houses. In two houses (A and B), only the feature and burial sherds were used; in three others (F, G, and H), both the feature and burial sherds and overlying plow zone sherds were used; and in one (K), only the sherds from the overlying plow zone were used.

Taking all ceramic types together, Houses F, G, and H showed the greatest deviation from the overall populations; and for these houses, the feature and burial samples deviated more than the plow zone samples (Table 7). Taking all house areas together, the types Pisgah Check Stamped and Pisgah Plain showed the greatest devia-

Table 6. Percentage Distribution of Pisgah Ceramic Types at the Warren Wilson Site.

HOUSE	CONTEXT	PERCENTAGES OF IDENTIFIED SHERDS					TOTAL IDENTIFIED SHERDS	UNIDENTIFIED SHERDS	GRAND TOTAL
		Rect. Comp.	Curv. Comp.	Check	Plain	Other			
A	F & B	87.1	0	4.3	8.6	0	93	27	120
B	F & B	89.7	0.8	3.2	6.3	0	126	125	251
F	PZ	85.4	2.1	11.4	1.1	0	726	602	1328
	F & B	80	3.9	15	1.1	0	180	110	290
G	PZ	86.4	2.6	10	1.0	0	1206	1325	2531
	F & B	65	1.7	26.6	6.7	0	60	47	107
H	PZ	90	1.0	9.0	0	0	441	408	849
	F & B	80.5	0	7.8	11.7	0	77	25	102
K	PZ	86.2	1.4	10.6	1.8	0	349	344	693
Plowzone (All)		88	1.7	9.0	1.2	0.1	14935	11084	26019
Feat. & Bur. (All)		86.6	1.4	8.2	3.7	0.1	2246	1916	4125

F = features
B = burials
PZ = plow zone

Table 7. Significance Tests of the Deviance from the Overall Ceramic Populations of Total Ceramics in Individual House Contexts.

HOUSE	CONTEXT	CHI SQUARE*	PROBABILITY OF RANDOMNESS
A	F & B	8.6756, df=3	.05>p>.02
B	F & B	6.5556, df=3	.1>p >.05
F	PZ	5.6223, df=3	.2>p>.1
	F & B	19.0771, df=3	p<.001
G	PZ	6.8158, df=3	.1>p >.05
	F & B	27.5348, df=3	p<.001
H	PZ	7.0427, df=3	.1>p >.05
	F & B	13.1032, df=3	p<.005
K	PZ	2.0064, df=3	.5>p>.3

* X^2 corrected for continuity when sherd sample size was less than 10.

F = features
B = burials
PZ = plow zone

tion from the overall populations. These types deviated more in the feature and burial samples than in the plow zone samples (Table 8). Finally, taking the feature and burial samples from the three most deviant houses (F, G, and H) together, the types Pisgah Check Stamped and Pisgah Plain were again the only types that deviated significantly from the overall populations (Table 9).

Any meaningful interpretations of variances in house-related ceramics at the Warren Wilson site will have to await more secure determinations of changes in overall settlement pattern and the analysis of additional house samples. The frequencies observed in the above analyses may have temporal or social meaning, but any such interpretations at this point would have to be tentative. For example, Houses F, G, and H (the structures with the most deviant ceramics) are all located close together in the northwestern portion of the excavated village area. The unexpectedly high proportions of checked and plain pottery in the fill of burials and features in these three structures might be interpreted as preference for those styles by a specific social unit within the village. The greater deviations overall in samples from feature and burial fill are expected since these samples represent short-term deposition and would have been subjected to much less mixing than the samples from the overlying plow zone.

CHRONOLOGICAL POSITION

In western North Carolina, the relative chronological position of Pisgah ceramics is well established. They are preceded by Connestee series and are followed by the Qualla series. At some sites in northeastern Tennessee, deposits containing Pisgah sherds are mixed with or overlain by deposits containing Dallas sherds (Richard Polhemus, personal communication).

At the present, there are only a few radiocarbon dates, and some of these have tenuous Pisgah associations. Charcoal from a pit containing Pisgah refuse (including 958 Pisgah sherds) at the Garden Creek Mound, Haywood County, North Carolina, was radiocarbon dated at A.D. 1435 ± 70 (GX0595). The pit probably was dug for the acquisition of subsoil clay used in building either Mound Floor 1 or Mound Floor 2, both of which were constructed in the late Pisgah phase. Several sherds from this pit displayed attributes, such as curvilinear complicated stamping and bold check stamping, that are

Table 8. Significance Tests of the Deviance from the Overall Ceramic Populations of Individual Ceramic Types in Collective House Contexts.

CERAMIC TYPE	CONTEXT	CHI SQUARE*	PROBABILITY OF RANDOMNESS
REC. COMP. STP.	ALL HOUSE PZ	3.800, df=3	.95>p>.9
	ALL HOUSE F & B	1.9973, df=4	.8>p>.7
CURV. COMP. STP.	ALL PZ	4.2523, df=3	.3>p>.2
	ALL F & B	5.1787, df=4	.3>p>.2
CHECK STP.	ALL PZ	1.5052, df=3	.7>p>.5
	ALL F & B	22.6425, df=4	p<.001
PLAIN	ALL PZ	4.6920, df=3	p<.2
	ALL F & B	10.1030, df=4	.05>p>.02

* X^2 corrected for continuity when sherd sample size was less than 10.

F = features
B = burials
PZ = plow zone

Table 9. Significance Tests of the Deviance from the Overall Ceramic Population
of Individual Ceramic Types in the Features and Burials of the

Three Most Deviant Structures (Houses F, G, and H).

CERAMIC TYPE	CHI SQUARE*	PROBABILITY OF RANDOMNESS
REC. COMP. STP.	.8801	.7>p>.5
CURV. COMP. STP.	1.9003	.5>p>.3
CHECK STP.	6.5336	.05>p>.02
PLAIN	10.2909	.01>p>.001

* X^2 corrected for continuity when sherd sample size was less than 10.

F = features
B = burials
PZ = plow zone

considered to be transitional to Qualla styles.

There are three dates from the Chauga Mound, Oconee County, South Carolina, where small numbers of Pisgah sherds were found throughout the excavations (Kelly and Neitzel 1961:64-66). Two of the dates, A.D. 830 ± 150 (M-933) and A.D. 880 ± 150 (M-934), appear to be too early for their contexts. A third determination, A.D. 1180 ± 150 (M-935), from Mound Stage 3, may be more nearly correct.

C. G. Holland (1970:61) reports a date of A.D. 1210 ± 120 (S-131) on charcoal from a depth of 12 to 18 inches in square "B" at Site 17 in Lee County, Virginia. The associated pottery consisted of only one Lee series (Pisgah) sherd and four New River series sherds.

Four dates from the Town Creek Mound (Pee Dee phase) in Montgomery County, North Carolina, are important, since small numbers of Pee Dee sherds have been found in direct association (in features) with Pisgah sherds at the Garden Creek and Warren Wilson sites. The Town Creek dates are A.D. 1205 ± 140 (FSU-174), A.D. 1280 ± 140 (FSU-176), A.D. 1350 ± 140 (FSU-145), and A.D. 1355 ± 50 (FSU-175) (Joffre Coe, personal communication).

The above dates, when combined with available dating on earlier and later ceramics, lead me to place Pisgah ceramics in the period ca. A.D. 1000-1450. On the basis of stylistic differences, a tentative subdivision can be made into an early subphase (ca. A.D. 1000-1250) and a late subphase (ca. A.D. 1250-1450). Most of the pottery from the Warren Wilson and Garden Creek sites seems to represent the late subphase.

AREAL RELATIONSHIPS

Pisgah vessel forms, paste characteristics, and surface finishes exhibit some ties to preceding Middle Woodland pottery of the Appalachian Summit. For instance, the earlier Connestee series (Keel 1972) contains a small percentage of sherds with complicated stamped designs that appear to be ancestral to Pisgah Rectilinear Complicated Stamped (Plate 64F-J). Ultimate origins for these designs may lie in the types Napier Stamped and Woodstock Stamped of northern Georgia (Wauchope 1966:57-63). Check stamping is also found in the preceding Connestee series (Keel 1972:133-141).

Stamped motifs on early (ca. A.D. 1000-1250) Pisgah ceramics (Plate 62D, G) exhibit definite resemblances to the small, angular complicated stamps on Etowah pottery (Wauchope 1966:64-77) of the Southern Piedmont region. This relationship to more southerly pottery styles continued in the period ca. A.D. 1250-1450, during which time Pisgah potters adopted bolder and more varied complicated stamps and some new rim treatments. Counterparts are found in the Savannah/Wilbanks series (Wauchope 1966:76-79; Sears 1958:129-194), Pee Dee series (Coe 1952:301-311; Reid 1967:12-25; Plate 65B-D), and Dan River series (Coe and Lewis 1952; Plate 65A). Some Pisgah rim sherds (Plate 63P, S) of this same period have incised decorations and appendages that resemble Dallas styles (Lewis and Kneberg 1946:105), and some sherds from sites on the Clinch and Holston rivers are tempered with crushed shell (Polhemus and Polhemus 1966:20). On the eastern mountain fringes, a relationship to the Burke series (Keeler 1971) is indicated by the presence of Pisgah sherds with steatite temper (Plate 65H).

By A.D. 1400-1450, Pisgah ceramic styles seem to have become limited primarily to the mountain basins of western North Carolina and northwestern South Carolina. A continuation of strong influence from the south is evidenced by the introduction of styles of the Lamar series (Wauchope 1966:79-87; Plate 64A). Incorporation of Lamar styles into the repertoire of Pisgah potters, accomplished by around A.D. 1450, produced the styles of the Qualla series. Qualla pottery has been identified with the historic Middle Cherokees (Egloff 1967).

At present, no antecedent forms can be found in the Appalachian Summit, or in closely neighboring areas, for the thickened and collared rims (and accompanying decorative elements) of Pisgah pottery. Kelly and Neitzel (1961) have suggested a relationship to northern Iroquoian ceramics, and some parallels can be observed in late prehistoric ceramics of western New York state and southeastern Ontario, where there are collared rims with oblique-angle incised patterns, notched strips, vertical lugs, and small castellations (MacNeish 1952:Plates IV, V, VIII). MacNeish (1952:82,87) proposes that these traits developed out of Owasco ceramics in the period A.D. 1100-1350.

Pottery of the Anderson focus (Fort Ancient Aspect) in southwestern Ohio also exhibits rim treatments similar to Pisgah. There are thickened rims decorated with angled punctations, punctated strap handles, notched lugs, and notched appliqued strips (Griffin 1966:107-118).

The most convincing similarities to Pisgah rim styles that I have observed are found in pottery of the Oliver phase in central and southern Indiana (Griffin 1966; Dorwin 1971).[4] Bowen Collared: Straight Variety (Dorwin 1971:267-268 and Plates XXIV-XXVII), for example, has a collared rim that is decorated with rows of impressions made with the edge of a cord wrapped paddle. These impressions sometimes form open-ended chevrons, as on Pisgah rims. Vertical lugs, castellations, notched rim strips, and handles may also be present. Griffin (1966:261-267) expresses the view that Oliver pottery was basically a Late Woodland product, but that it also was influenced by Fort Ancient and possibly by Iroquois ceramic styles. Dorwin (1971:382-383) places the Oliver phase between A.D. 800-1300, with a supporting radiocarbon date of A.D. 1060 ± 100 (M-2010) from the Oliver site.

At this time, it seems most probable that collared pot rims and accompanying decorations were introduced into the southern Appalachians from the Midwest, perhaps along a broad frontier of expanding Mississippian culture. Dorwin (1971:383-390) has suggested that these cultures were receptive to, and readily exchanged, new ideas and techniques. To test this hypothesis, further data are needed from eastern Kentucky, southwestern Virginia, and northeastern Tennessee.

RELATIONSHIPS OF PISGAH CERAMICS TO HISTORIC CHEROKEE CERAMICS

In 1961, Joffre Coe provided a brief description of Pisgah ceramic traits and noted that "these characteristics appear on pottery that seems to be ancestral to that used by at least some of the historic Cherokee" (Coe 1961:59). Recent investigations in western North Carolina support the view that Pisgah ceramic styles merged with generalized Lamar styles in the period around A.D. 1400-1450 to produce Qualla series ceramics. Although developed Qualla styles are distinctly different from Pisgah styles, some persistent Pisgah traits are recognizable. These include basic vessel forms, burnished vessel interiors, check stamps, the use of ladder-like complicated stamps, the application of notched rim strips, and certain rim decorations.

Qualla sherds were found by Egloff (1967) in high proportions

4. I am grateful to James Kellar and John Dorwin for permission to examine Oliver pottery from their excavations in central Indiana.

(45 to 98 percent) in collections from historically documented Cherokee Middle, Valley, and Out towns. He also found relatively large amounts (14 to 55 percent) in collections from the Lower towns, and minor amounts (3 to 16 percent) in the Overhill towns. Many of Egloff's sites, especially the Middle and Out towns, also contained Pisgah sherds. Vessels with attributes clearly transitional between Pisgah and Qualla were found at Garden Creek Mound No. 1.

On the basis of these observations, there seems to be little doubt that Pisgah pottery was an important component in the lineage leading to historic Cherokee ceramics. This relationship was strongest in the area of the Middle, Valley, and Out towns, but it was also important in the Lower Town area. In the Overhill area, the legacy of Pisgah ceramics is at present unclear. Nevertheless, the abundance of early Pisgah sherds on some sites along the Clinch, Holston, and lower French Broad rivers (frequently underlying or mixed with Dallas sherds) provides grounds for questioning a late (protohistoric or historic) migration of the Cherokees into eastern Tennessee, as proposed by Webb (1938) and Lewis and Kneberg (1946).

The present data, especially the evidence of strong influence upon Qualla ceramics from the more southerly Lamar styles, partly support Sears' (1955:147) suggestion that Cherokee pottery styles "developed in the Underhill area and later spread to the north." However, this interpretation does not take into consideration the existence of an indigenous ceramic tradition in the Appalachian Summit, nor of the part played specifically by Pisgah potters in the development of Qualla styles.

6. Food Remains

Food remains, in the forms of animal bones, charred vegetal materials, and occasional mollusk shells, were found in Pisgah contexts at the Warren Wilson and Garden Creek sites. These remains were most abundant in the fill of features and post molds. Concentrations of refuse sometimes indicated the disposal of a single large mass of garbage, but usually the material was scattered in the fill. The pit fill of burials seldom contained food refuse, except occasionally in the upper portion where it had collected after the pit fill had settled. The plow zone at both sites also contained food remains, but since these remains had been disturbed and subjected to modern contamination, there was no effort to recover them beyond sifting through ½-inch screens.

In the work at the Warren Wilson and Garden Creek sites, pit fill was carefully processed in order to retrieve small artifacts and food remains. The soil was first washed through a screen having 1.3-mm mesh, and afterward the charcoal was separated by flotation. At the Warren Wilson site, most of the screening was done at a facility set up near the site. Samples were then carried to the laboratory in Chapel Hill where the plant remains were separated by flotation.

FAUNAL REMAINS

Ten samples of animal bone from the Warren Wilson excavations were examined by Elizabeth Wing. Included were the remains from Features 7, 53, 57, 136, and 137; Burials 3 and 7 (pit fill); a 25-foot section of Palisade D; a group of post molds associated with House E; and a plow zone sample from one 10-foot square. The plow zone sample, obtained by sifting through ½-inch-mesh screens, was submitted for comparison with the fine-screened samples. Dr. Wing's list of identified species by minimum number of individual animals, along with her preliminary observations, is found in Appendix 2.

The identifications indicate that a wide range of faunal resources was exploited by the Pisgah villagers. Animals were hunted and collected for their meat primarily, but also for their bones, skins, and fur. Certain "incidental" species—mice, small birds, snakes, and toads—probably represent village pests. Large mammals (deer and bear) were important for their meat, but small mammals, birds, amphibians, and fish (and possibly some of the incidental species) also were eaten. Aquatic species were only about one-fourth as important to subsistence as terrestrial species. Buffalo *(Bison bison)* and elk *(Cervus canadensis),* of which at least one individual each was tentatively identified at the Garden Creek site (Joffre Coe, personal communication), were not present in the Warren Wilson samples.

Dr. Wing points out the relative abundance of bones of rodents, small birds, and snakes in Features 7 and 57. As noted in Chapter 2, Feature 7 consisted of a garbage-filled depression along the route of a palisade, and Feature 57 was interpreted as the subsurface floor of a sweat house. The presence of bones of "incidental" animals in both of these features is expected since these types of animals would have been attracted to the garbage heap and would have made their homes in the structure after its abandonment.

It is likely that smaller bones would have been lost on the house floors, and consequently would have become trapped in the depressions over burial pits, whereas larger bones would have been removed with other garbage. Therefore, although burial pits do not appear to have been used as garbage repositories, the occurrence of bones of small animals in the upper portions of the pit fill is predictable.

The relative abundance of the bones of fur-bearing mammals in the total collection has suggested to Dr. Wing the possibility that these animals were hunted as much for their fur as for their meat.

The distributions of species by house area (B, C, D, and E) are of little value at the present stage in the work at Warren Wilson. However, after the bone collections from additional house areas have been analyzed and after more information has been acquired on the chronological relationships of the structures on the site, it may be possible to interpret temporal variations in subsistence practices.

PLANT REMAINS

Charred plant remains from six features at the Warren Wilson site —Features 7, 56, 57, 136, 137, and 140—were analyzed by Richard

Yarnell. All of the charcoal from these features, except for small
amounts retained for radiocarbon dating, was submitted. Dr. Yarnell's report, together with a quantified list of identified plants, is
found in Appendix 1. Patricia Sanford (1970) studied two additional samples from the Warren Wilson site, one from Feature 141 and
another from Feature 146, both excavated in 1969. Feature 141
consisted of a thick, stratified midden along the bank on the eastern
and southeastern margins of the site, and Feature 146 represented a
large refilled storage pit.

In Yarnell's samples, cultigens were represented by corn, squash
(or pumpkin), beans, and sumpweed. Wild plant foods were represented by hickory nuts, acorns, walnuts, and butternuts, as well as
several fruits and possibly some small seeds. In overall quantity,
nutshells were most abundant, followed by cultigens, then fruits,
and finally seeds, the latter being poorly represented. Yarnell sus-
pects that corn and possibly beans, squash, and sumpweed were underrepresented because of their fragility and poor preservation on
an open site. The importance of these cultigens to the economy,
therefore, may have been greater than indicated by their quantities
in the analyzed samples.

In the samples examined by Sanford, corn was the only cultigen.
Carbonized remains of wild plants included maypop seeds and unidentified nut fragments. A large group of noncarbonized seeds that
may not be archaeological included, in order of frequency, *Galium*
sp., *Amaranthus* sp., *Chenopodium* sp., Aster family, *Polygonum*
sp., *Oxalis stricta, Eleusine indica,* and *Taraxacum officinale.*

Corn fragments in the samples analyzed by Yarnell and Sanford
were of the Eastern Complex, eight-row (and possibly ten-row) variety. Corn fragments have also been recognized in the charcoal from
various features at Garden Creek Mound No. 1, but analysis of these
specimens has not yet been made.

Recent studies by Yarnell (1972:335-341) have assigned the
sumpweed seeds from the Warren Wilson site to an extinct variety,
Iva annua var. *macrocarpa.* This, Yarnell believes, is an extinct cultivated variety that had a habitat range far to the east of its original
progenitors and of the modern wild varieties.

Most of the identified cultigens and wild plants are harvestable in
summer and autumn, but the presence of other types of food resources, along with a stockaded village, permanent houses, and food
storage pits, attests to the probability of year-round occupancy of
the site. The great abundance of wood charcoal, which Yarnell

points out as being reminiscent of northern sites or winter occupations, might be explained by the fact that features with the largest amounts of charcoal were purposely picked for analysis. Thus, there may have been a bias toward autumn or winter features.

7. Summary and Conclusions

A recurring complex of archaeological remains from numerous sites in the Southern Appalachians has been termed the Pisgah phase. In the preceding pages, these remains have been described in terms of sites, structures, features, burials, artifacts, ceramics, and food residue. Materials from the two most extensively excavated Pisgah sites—Warren Wilson and Garden Creek—seem mostly to represent a late subphase that can be dated to approximately A.D. 1250-1450. An early subphase, defined primarily by ceramic styles, is estimated to date A.D. 1000-1250.

Pisgah sites have been found throughout an area of about 14,000 square miles in the South Appalachian province. The greatest number of known sites is located in the heart of the Appalachian Summit region, on the headwaters of the Holston, Nolichucky, Tuckasegee, Pigeon, French Broad, Little Tennessee, Catawba, Saluda, and Keowee rivers. In addition, there is a scattering of sites to the west and north, along the Hiwassee, lower French Broad, Clinch, Powell, and other rivers.

Many of the sites on the periphery of the Appalachian Summit appear to have been occupied mainly in the early subphase, or for relatively short periods of time. In the interior of the region, some sites contain evidence of having been occupied throughout the phase, while others—such as the Warren Wilson and Garden Creek sites—seem to have been occupied primarily in the late subphase. Sites vary in size from about ¼ acre to about 6 acres, the more spacious portions of alluvial valleys being the favored locations for settlement. The Warren Wilson site probably is representative of a medium-sized village that at first covered about ½ acre but was later enlarged by stages to include about 3 acres.

Houses were constructed of upright posts, had a square to slightly rectangular plan (about 20 feet on a side), a depressed floor, a central platform hearth, and a vestibule entrance. These houses probably were walled with bark or woven mats and were roofed with bark or straw thatch. The house floors, and areas immediately surrounding the houses, contained burials, clay borrow pits, storage pits, and additional fire basins. The villages probably also contained sweat houses, storage cribs, and other small structures. The houses and other structures were arranged around a plaza, and the whole complex was enclosed by a defensive palisade. An entrance to the village, at least in its early stages, was formed by an offset in the palisade, at the point of easiest access to the nearby river.

Although only limited excavations were conducted in the two village areas at the Garden Creek site, it appears that these settlements were much larger than the Warren Wilson village. Adjacent middens covered about 4 and 5 acres, respectively. In addition to their larger size, these villages also contained platform mounds. In the smaller village area, a substructure mound had been initiated in the Connestee phase of the late Middle Woodland period and was reused by the later Pisgah occupants. In the second and slightly larger village area, which in an early stage had been surrounded by a palisade with rectangular bastions, there was an elaborate sequence of ceremonial/civic constructions. Initially there were two conjoined earth lodges adjacent to a large, probably arborlike structure. Eventually, the latter structure was demolished and covered by a pavement of river boulders. Following this, the boulders, and finally the earth lodges themselves, were covered with earth fill and a clay cap to form a large flat-topped mound. This mound underwent a series of enlargements, with a new structure (similar to the village houses) on each surface. Its final use was in the Qualla phase.

At the Warren Wilson site, human burials were found in the house floors or immediately adjacent to the houses. In some cases, there was evidence that a hearth had been removed to make way for a burial at the center of the house floor, after which a new hearth was constructed over the burial pit. At Garden Creek, there were also burials in the mound floors. Pisgah phase burials were made in either simple pits, side-chamber pits, or central-chamber pits, with the central-chamber form possibly being older than the side-chamber form. There is also evidence that the side-chamber form was reserved for infants and male adults of high rank. A body was usually placed in the pit in a loosely flexed position with the head to the west, perhaps with an intentional orientation toward the location of other important sites or groups of sites. All of the adult skulls were artificially flattened at the forehead and occiput.

Columella shell beads were included in the burials of adults and infants. Adults also were adorned with shell ear pins, shell bowls, turtle shell rattles, and perforated animal bones. Infants were the most frequent recipients of shell gorgets and perforated *Marginella* shells. At the Warren Wilson site, grave goods were found with burials in certain houses, but were lacking in burials associated with other houses. This difference may be evidence for social stratification, an interpretation which has some support in the apparent greater overall frequency of grave goods in the mound burials at Garden Creek than in the village burials at Warren Wilson.

Artifacts of the Pisgah phase were made from stone, clay, bone, shell, and wood. Chipped stone implements consisted of small triangular projectile points and an assortment of small flake tools. Ground stone was represented by rectanguloid celts, small discs, elbow pipes, and pottery burnishing stones. Pecked stone implements consisted of hammerstones, anvil stones, mortars, and manos. A fourth category, cut stone, consisted of mica and various pigment stones such as hematite, limonite, graphite, and ocher. There is abundant evidence in the Appalachian Summit for aboriginal mica mining, and it is possible that the Pisgah peoples traded this material for marine shell and other exotic goods.

Clay artifacts consisted of small elbow pipes, discs made from potsherds, beads in a variety of shapes, animal figurines, and miniature pottery vessels. Bone tools, represented by awls and other pointed implements, were made from sections of long bones and small bone splinters from deer and turkey. There were also ornamental bone pins, turtle shell rattles, and beads of animal bone.

Marine mollusks served as the raw material for various burial-related artifacts. Large spheroidal beads were made from the conch columella, and small tubular and disc beads were made from the outer wall of conch shells. The large columella beads were worn as either necklaces or bracelets, while the small beads appear to have been worn only as necklaces. Ear pins were also made from the conch columella, and sometimes intact conch shells were used as ritual containers. Circular gorgets, made from the conch wall, were engraved and excised with representations of a coiled rattlesnake with "forked eye," or in one case with a stylized dancer motif. Another form of gorget was a cross or quadrilobed square. Perforated *Marginella* shells were sometimes sewn to the garments in which infants were buried.

The Pisgah ceramic series can be organized into four types—Pisgah Rectilinear Complicated Stamped, Pisgah Curvilinear Complicated Stamped, Pisgah Check Stamped, and Pisgah Plain. In addition, pots were occasionally finished with woven-reed (or quill), corncob, cord, or net impressions. Within the rectilinear stamped category, there were three design variations, the most common of which was an arrangement of several parallel vertical lines flanked on either side by a series of shorter horizontal lines. This design was stamped in succession to form a series of ladder-like patterns. Two less common variations had either the horizontal or the vertical elements slanted, so that when stamped in succession they formed a herringbone-like pattern. There were two rarely occurring curvilinear designs, one with pairs of concentric circles separated by a single-line element and another with interlocking scrolls. In most collections, rectilinear stamped was dominant, followed by check stamped, then by plain, and finally by curvilinear stamped.

The basic vessel form was a globular jar with an everted rim and a collar. Thickened rims, straight rims, and inslanted rims also occurred. Rim decorations consisted of rows of diagonal punctations, or occasionally, incised patterns. Rim appendages, such as loop handles, nodes, vertical lugs, and appliqued strips, were common. Shallow bowls usually were decorated with a thin, pinched or notched strip around the rim. Pottery clay was frequently tempered with fine-to-coarse sand, occasionally with crushed quartz, or rarely with shell (only in Tennessee) or steatite (only along the eastern border of the Blue Ridge), and there was usually a large amount of mica in the clay. The exteriors of vessels were light gray to buff in color, the interior dark gray to black.

The origins of the thickened and collared rims are enigmatic, as they do not seem to have antecedents in the Southern Appalachians. Some reasonably close parallels can be found in the vessel forms of Oliver phase pottery in central and southern Indiana, and it is probable that the collared vessel form was introduced to the Pisgah area from the northwest, along a frontier of expanding Mississippian culture, around A.D. 1000.

Beginning around A.D. 1250, Pisgah potters were affected by the first in a continuing series of interactions with cultures to the south and west, which brought about the use of more varied and bolder rectilinear stamps, some curvilinear stamps, larger vessels, small vertical lugs to replace loop handles, and an inslanted, cazuela-like rim with incised decorations. By about A.D. 1400, Pisgah ceramic styles, now limited to the interior of the Appalachian Summit, began to take on an increasing number of attributes of the more southerly Lamar development. A merger of Lamar and Pisgah styles, accomplished by about A.D. 1450, resulted in the Qualla series pottery, which has been identified with historically documented Cherokee towns.

The Pisgah subsistence economy appears to have been based on approximately equal parts hunting, gathering, and agriculture. Eastern Complex corn was cultivated by the Pisgah occupants of both the Warren Wilson and the Garden Creek sites, and its presence in each of seven refuse samples from Warren Wilson suggests that it was of major importance to the economy. Other cultigens identified in the Warren Wilson samples were squash (or pumpkins), beans, and sumpweed. Wild plant foods—nuts, fruits, and small seeds (in that order)—were about equally as important as cultivated plant foods. The remains of mammals, birds, snakes, amphibians, and fish were identified at the Warren Wilson site, and it is probable that these animals were hunted and collected for their bones, carapaces, hides, and fur, in addition to their meat. White-tailed deer and wild turkey were the most important food animals.

CONCLUDING REMARKS

The Pisgah phase represents the development in the Appalachian Summit of a primarily Mississippian cultural pattern. Such traits as small triangular arrow points, polished stone celts and discs, clay elbow pipes and discs, marine shell grave goods, palisaded villages, platform mounds, complicated stamped ceramics, and maize agriculture are representative of this new pattern. Other Mississippian traits, such as shell tempered pottery and extended burials, common to the Tennessee Valley and the Southern Piedmont, are missing.

However, simply to list the presence or absence of traits is of little explanatory value. Even though Pisgah sites have permanent houses, palisades, and platform mounds, they are not identical to their counterparts to the south and west. For example, the Garden Creek site obviously was an important center in its day, but it does not compare in size and complexity with centers in the Tennessee Valley, such as Hiwassee Island, or in the Southern Piedmont, such as Etowah. Larson (1971) has proposed that Etowah was the administrative and redistributional center for a powerful chiefdom, and Sears (1968) has made Etowah and other similar Southeastern sites the seats for priest states having an "upper class or caste" as proprietors of a "state cult." While I believe that the Garden Creek site and possibly other mound sites of the Pisgah phase were the forerunners of the "town centers" of the historic Cherokees, I am not convinced that they were the foci of chiefdoms or states.

This interpretation is supported by the apparent lack of a well-defined elite mortuary paraphernalia in the Pisgah phase. Both Sears (1968) and Larson (1971) emphasize the importance of such paraphernalia in the validation and reinforcement of elite rights and statuses. Although there was a slightly higher percentage of burials with accompanying artifacts at Garden Creek Mound No. 1 than at the Warren Wilson village, there was little difference in the types of grave goods or amounts per burial. This can be contrasted with the distinctive Southern Cult material and specialized mortuary pottery found in elite burials of the Etowah-Wilbanks and Dallas cultures. This is not to say that there are no status distinctions represented in Pisgah burial associations (the probability for this has already been established), but there does not seem to be a specific set of items confined to a small elite group.

Also, there almost certainly were some differences in economic and demographic patterns between the Pisgah, Etowah-Wilbanks, and Dallas cultures. The Ridge and Valley province, where most Dallas sites are found, and the Southern Blue Ridge and Piedmont provinces, where most Etowah-Wilbanks sites are found, are characterized by broad and lengthy alluvial valleys, which would provide for substantial agricultural productivity and for the aggregation of large populations. In most of the Appalachian Summit, however, flood plains are more restricted in size and in gross agricultural potential. Preliminary analyses of Pisgah food remains suggest broad-range, localized subsistence exploitation, as opposed to a highly specialized agricultural base, and the settlement data point to rather small population aggregates. If, as Service (1962:146-147) has proposed, a food surplus for redistribution is necessary in the maintenance of a chiefdom, the Ridge and Valley and Piedmont areas would have been more promising for this type of social structure.

Aside from these possible differences in social structure and economy, the Pisgah people and neighboring Mississippian peoples seem, nevertheless, to have had specific ties in material culture. From the available comparative data, these material correspondences seem to have been strongest between Pisgah and the Dallas phase of eastern Tennessee, the Etowah and Wilbanks phases of northern Georgia, the Pee Dee phase of the Carolina Piedmont, the

Savannah phase of the Carolina Coastal Plain, and the Woodside phase of southeastern Kentucky.

Again, however, indiscriminate trait comparisons have little meaning. In order to estimate the extent of allegiances and interaction between the Pisgah and neighboring cultures, heavier weight should be given to those traits that presumably would have had greater sensitivity to social and ideological trends. For instance, the chipping patterns and basic forms of stone tools, dictated primarily by technofunctional considerations, would be expected to have a low social and ideological load. Pottery traits, on the other hand, especially decorative features, would be expected to have a high sociological load. And finally, mortuary traits, such as patterns of burial offerings, would be expected to have strong social and ideological loads, and little if any technofunctional load.[1]

Following these precepts, certain traits can be assigned greater weight in evaluating the sociopolitical ties between Pisgah and other South Appalachian cultures. It is more significant that some of the phases mentioned shared the same shell gorget style than that some of them shared similar pottery styles, and the pottery styles are more important than the fact that all of the phases had a common small triangular projectile point. Likewise, I would weigh traits of ceremonial/civic architecture more heavily than traits of domestic architecture.

When all traits are considered and greater weight is assigned to those traits that carry a greater social and ideological load, the Pisgah phase appears to have strongest connections to the Dallas and Wilbanks phases. For example, all three have ceremonial earth lodges, the Lick Creek gorget style, and chambered burials. But there are some major differences: the Wilbanks culture participated more directly than the other two in the Southern Cult, and the Dallas culture participated more directly in the Middle Mississippian ceramic tradition. In late Pisgah, at least, the overall strongest connections seem to be with Dallas, the major difference being in ceramics. Some years ago, Coe (1961:59) suggested that the differences between the Appalachian Summit cultures and those of the Tennessee Valley were of "degree rather than kind," and he was not surprised to find dissimilarity in the ceramics of the two areas, since the Tennessee Valley was "closest to and first to come under the influence of the Mississippian type cultures."

1. These levels are essentially the same as Binford's (1962) "technomic," "sociotechnic," and "ideotechnic" categories.

An explanation for the existence of significant ceramic differences between Dallas and Pisgah, alongside other very comparable traits, might be drawn from comparative ethnography. If the late prehistoric South Appalachian cultures were clan exogamous and matrilocal in marital residence, as they were historically, then differential distribution of certain traits within the broader social setting would be expected (Deetz 1967:94-96). For example, if we can assume on ethnohistorical grounds that the women were the potters and that they were, as a result of matrilocality, less mobile in the overall social setting than males, then it is likely that female-related traits—such as ceramic styles—would have had more localized distribution. Likewise, if we can make a somewhat less secure assumption that traits related to ceremonial/civic architecture, shell working, and mortuary activities were male-related, then because of the male's greater mobility in the overall social setting, we would expect such traits to have had a broader areal distribution. These latter traits, however, would still have been limited primarily to the boundaries of maximum sociopolitical allegiances. All of this, which I admit is highly conjectural, has some bearing on the problem of defining the boundaries of emergent Cherokee society.

The Pisgah archaeological assemblage is found primarily within the area of the historic Cherokee Middle towns. In this area, there are many "carry-over" traits from the Pisgah phase to the Qualla phase, which is definitely Cherokee. But, again, in evaluating the possible behavioral correlates of these archaeological continuities, I would weigh certain traits more heavily than others. Consequently, I find in the persistence from Pisgah to Qualla of a comparable inventory of grave goods, of chambered burial pits, of earth-covered ceremonial structures, and of a related gorget style strong evidence for a persistent social tradition. The prehistoric distribution of Pisgah traits, however, is not limited to the Middle Cherokee area. It extends to the north and west, into parts of the area occupied historically by the Overhill Cherokees, and to the south, into parts of the historic Lower Cherokee territory. In the former area, Pisgah ceramic styles were replaced in the 14th century by Dallas styles; in the latter area, Pisgah styles formed small to moderate components in predominantly Etowah and Wilbanks assemblages. Even though Pisgah ceramic styles may not have remained intact as long, or even have represented a dominant theme, in the other areas, I do feel that the Pisgah culture played a part—perhaps through the sharing of certain socially and ideologically meaningful traits—in the ultimate synthesis of the historic cultural patterns in those areas.

I suggest, therefore, that the Pisgah, Etowah-Wilbanks, and Dallas phases formed vital strains in the development and ultimate synthesis of Cherokee Indian culture. Although ceramic styles appear to have been strongly affected by local factors, complicated stamping was an important component in this development. But even the differences that we find in the ceramics of the three phases are no greater than the material differences found in the respective subcultures of the Middle, Lower, and Overhill Cherokee settlements in the historic period. Finally, we might perceive in such traits as rattlesnake gorgets, chambered burials, and ceremonial earth lodges the material manifestations of an emergent Cherokee tradition. In fact, the geographic distribution of these traits is not unlike that of Cherokee settlements in the early historic period.

Appendixes

APPENDIX A

PLANT REMAINS FROM THE WARREN WILSON SITE

Richard A. Yarnell

The plant remains from the Warren Wilson site which were analyzed consist of 1,334 grams of material recovered by fine screening and flotation from six pits associated with house floors. Quantities per feature range from 30 to 419 grams. Of the total, 949 grams are a residue of fragments passing through a screen with 2.4 mm openings. Small seeds, small snails, fish scale fragments, bone fragments, and flint chips were recovered from the residue. Otherwise, the reported remains are from the 385 grams remaining, all of which were quantified. All but 6 grams of the quantified remains is carbonized plant material, of which 81 percent is wood charcoal and 14 percent is presumed food remains. Analysis of the plant food remains indicates that the diet of the occupants of the site included considerable quantities of corn, hickory nuts, and acorns, and lesser quantities of beans, squash or pumpkin, sumpweed seeds (marsh elder), walnuts, butternuts, and several kinds of fleshy fruit. Various carbonized weed seeds were identified also, but their dietary significance was probably slight if they were eaten at all. Quantified results are presented in Table A-1.

The great abundance of wood charcoal is reminiscent of northern sites. This may be because the elevation of the Warren Wilson site is relatively high or because primarily winter occupation is represented. Otherwise, the best indicators of season of occupation are the fruit seeds: persimmon, grape, and maypop (*Passiflora incarnata*). Persimmons are generally inedible until autumn, which is also the grape season. Maypops, however, are available from midsummer to autumn and probably are the least storable food represented and thus the best indicator of season of occupation. As usual, late summer and autumn are indicated by the wild plant foods, and summer and autumn are indicated by the cultigens. Thus, we have no evidence from the plant remains to oppose an inference that the site was occupied throughout the year.

As a result of identification of many of the larger pieces of wood charcoal, it appears that the vegetation in the vicinity of the site was dominated by pine and oak. Quantification was not attempted except in a very rough way, as in-

Table A-1. Plant Remains from the Warren Wilson Site.

FEATURE	7	56	57	136	137	140	TOTALS	PERCENT
Total weight in grams	217.5	269.8	314.2	419.4	82.4	30.4	1333.7	
Residue	165.7	227.0	210.0	277.8	48.1	20.3	948.9	71.15
Stone	0.14	1.25	0.53	0.28	0.06	x	2.26	0.17
Coal	0.06	0.01	x				0.07	x
Flint chips	0.08	0.04	0.05				0.17	0.01
Bone	0.66	0.96	0.60	0.99	0.06	0.32	3.59	0.27
Fish scale	x	0.01	0.01	0.01			0.03	x
Small snails	x	0.03	x	x	x		0.03	x
Plant remains	50.85	40.53	102.99	140.27	34.22	9.79	378.65	28.39
Carb. wood	40.34	20.86	91.6	114.8	31.06	6.88	305.54	80.69
Cane	0.60	0.20	0.20	0.10		0.07	1.17	0.31
Unidentified	3.08	10.38	1.33	0.88	0.43	1.26	17.36	4.58
Weed seeds	0.04	0.05	0.13	0.20	0.01	0.01	0.44	0.12
Composite head			0.02	0.14			0.16	0.04
Plant food	6.79	9.04	9.71	24.15	2.72	1.57	53.98	14.26
Hickory nutshell	3.41	7.71	3.14	19.70	2.02	0.52	36.50	67.62
Walnut	0.41	0.13	0.54	0.13	0.17	0.07	1.45	2.69
Butternut	0.24	0.07		0.03			0.34	0.63
Acorn shell	0.07	0.14	0.77	0.55	0.06	0.12	1.71	5.58
Acorn meat	0.23	0.36	0.35	0.36			1.30	
Corn cupules	1.90	0.38	1.11	1.75	0.18	0.40	5.72	21.32
Corn kernels	0.30	0.24	3.41	1.39	0.16	0.29	5.79	
Squash rind			0.01	0.01			0.02	0.13
Squash seed			0.02	0.03			0.05	0.65
Beans			0.22	0.13			0.35	0.07
Sumpweed	0.??	0.01	0.03	0.01		0.17	0.04	0.07
	0.??	0.01	0.11	0.06	0.13	0.17	0.71	1.32

Table A-1 (continued)

FEATURE	7	56	57	136	137	140	TOTALS
Number of seeds							
Fruits:							
Persimmon	2						2
Maypops		1	1	1	1	13	17
Grape	8		2	9	4	2	25
Sumac?	1						1
"Kamp Mound"	5						5
Black cherry					1 NC		
Rubus	2 NC						
Weeds:							
Polygonum					1	1	2
Galium				1	1		2
Ragweed	4	1	2				7
Chenopod		1	1				2
Poke		2 NC	1 NC	1			1
Solanum?	1						1
Grass	2						2
Unidentified	12	6	26	18	4	12	78

NC = non-carbonized

dicated in Table A-2. Both the red and white oak groups are well represented. Beyond this only hickory and chestnut were identified more than tentatively but, surprisingly, only once each. Questionable identifications include locust and (or) honey locust, cherry, poplar, and birch. An unidentified diffuse porous wood is relatively abundant, but no trees other than pine and oak are represented in great abundance. The large quantity of hickory nut shell (two-thirds of all plant food remains) indicates a substantial number of hickory trees, and walnut shell and butternut shell indicate the presence of these trees. A single noncarbonized, dark-brown cherry pit *(Prunus serotina)* may be prehistoric.

Grape vines tend to grow near streams and forest edges. Otherwise the plants represented generally grow in open ground, especially on new or old garden plots. In addition to the cultigens, these plants include maypops, poke *(Phytolacca americana)*, knotweed or smartweed (trigonous seeded *Polygonum)*, cleavers *(Galium)*, common ragweed *(Ambrosia artemesiifolia)*, chenopod, a grass (two seeds, 2.4 x 1.3 x 1.0 mm carbonized), possibly a small flowered composite (eight dome-shaped discs, 4- to 10-mm diameter carbonized), probably a nightshade *(Solanum?)* and sumac (uncertain identifications), possibly blackberry or raspberry *(Rubus,* noncarbonized), and perhaps several plants represented by unidentified seeds, the majority of which are small and indistinctive.

Five large and quite distinctive seeds of a single type were found in the material from Feature 7. These are entered in Table A-1 under the label "Kamp Mound." In August 1963, I collected berry-like fruits and leaves from an herb, approximately 2 feet in height, growing at the center of the top of the Hopewellian Kamp Mound. This earth work is densely covered with large shrubs and small trees and is located on the west bank of the Illinois River in Calhoun County, Illinois. The seeds from this plant and those from Feature 7 are the same, but I have never noticed the plant or the seeds elsewhere.

As usual, many noncarbonized weed seeds were found in the samples. Ordinarily I do not report noncarbonized plant remains unless special circumstances seem to warrant it. Materials that are obviously recent occur in almost all samples of archaeological plant remains that are sent to me; and in most cases, plant remains that occur carbonized are different from the noncarbonized remains. A major exception is *Chenopodium.* Two carbonized chenopod seeds were found in the Warren Wilson flotation samples along with over one hundred noncarbonized chenopod seeds, many of which appear to be relatively fresh, a few freshly germinated. It cannot be assumed that any but the two carbonized seeds are contemporary with the site occupation, and it is likely that they originated from incidental weeds, perhaps allowed to grow in garden plots and eaten as greens. Poke and cleavers may have been utilized in this way also.

Common ragweed seeds frequently occur in some abundance in samples of archaeological plant remains but usually are not carbonized. Nevertheless, only the seven carbonized achenes can safely be assumed to be contemporaneous

Table A-2. Carbonized Wood from the Warren Wilson Site.

Feature	Pine	Red Oak Group	White Oak Group	Locust or Honey Locust?	Cherry?	Other
7	2	1	3	1	1	
56	3	1	2	1	1	conifer
57	2	2	1	1	1	
136	3	2	1	1	1	hickory
137	2	1	1			chestnut
140	2	1	1	1		birch? poplar?

3 = very abundant
2 = abundant
1 = present

with the Warren Wilson occupation. The many noncarbonized achenes are too likely to be intrusive. The same interpretation is appropriate for the single carbonized seed and many noncarbonized seeds of the tentatively identified nightshade and also for poke with one seed carbonized and three not carbonized. Identified seeds in the samples with no carbonized representatives include flat-seeded *Polygonum* (many), nodding spurge *(Euphorbia maculata,* few), amaranth (few), and unidentified legumes and grasses (few). *Galium* and trigonous seeded *Polygonum* are not represented by noncarbonized seeds. Thus there is apparently a considerable representation of modern weeds and also weeds contemporaneous with aboriginal occupation at the site. The lack of complete overlap between them may indicate that the effects of aboriginal disturbance were in some ways different from the effects of modern disturbance. However, the difference may be one of degree rather than kind. I hope that this discussion adequately indicates the value of floristic surveys of archaeological sites before and during excavation.

The largest areas of disturbed ground probably were the dwelling sites and the garden plots which may have been together in one area. Mississippian sites tend to be located on relatively fertile and easily cultivated sandy loam soils in river valleys or near major streams. The abundant evidence of cultigens in the Warren Wilson plant remains indicates that the people who lived there were in a relatively good agricultural situation. Corn is represented in the plant food remains in quantity second only to hickory nut. However, it is likely that corn was more significant to subsistence since it is much more likely to be underrepresented in the carbonized plant remains. Beans, squash, and sumpweed *(Iva annua* var. *macrocarpa)* are probably underrepresented also. Altogether the cultigen remains are 22.2 percent of the total plant food remains. Nut remains constitute 76.5 percent of the total and fruit seeds only 1.3 percent. However, the fruits probably contributed major amounts of certain vitamins, especially vitamin C. Various beverages made from plant products also would be significant if not essential vitamin contributors, but archaeological evidence for beverages, like tubers and greens, rarely is found.

Acorn, like the cultigens, is probably considerably underrepresented in the plant food remains. This is suspected because of the high proportion of oak in the wood charcoal and because acorn shell, being relatively delicate when carbonized, is less likely to be preserved and recovered than hickory nut shell. In addition, the amount of food represented by a given weight of acorn shell is much greater than for the same weight of hickory nut shell. Thus it appears that hickory nut, acorn, corn, and possibly also beans were the major plant foods at the Warren Wilson village, though not necessarily in this order of importance. My general impression is that food from the gardens and plant foods from elsewhere were somewhere nearly equal in the average year. Some years the intentionally cultivated crops would be especially productive, but other years the people would be forced to rely more heavily on the products of the natural vegetation. Fluctuations in the availability of various animal foods would further complicate annual subsistence variation.

The corn grown is apparently what has been called Northern Flint and Eastern Complex. The few whole kernels found have the characteristic broad, low shape with embryos detached. Cob is represented almost entirely by individual cupules. However, one small cob section apparently had formed part of an eight-row or ten-row ear.

The most surprising items to appear in the samples were seeds of *Iva annua*. Like the sumpweed seeds from the Late Hopewellian Apple Creek site in Illinois, they are lacking the achene coats, though the Warren Wilson seeds are a little larger. Average measurements of the seven seeds are 4.6 x 3.5 mm. Adding approximately 0.7 x 0.4 mm. for the achene coat and 10 percent for shrinkage as a result of carbonization to each dimension, these figures become approximately 5.9 x 4.3 mm. This is about the size of the early Late Woodland achenes from the Stillwell site in Illinois where sumpweed probably was cultivated. Modern *Iva annua* achenes are only half as large as the Warren Wilson reconstructed average size, and the modern range of the species is primarily in the Mississippi Valley region and somewhat westward. The Warren Wilson *Iva* seeds are the most easterly of those so far discovered and thus are the ones farthest removed from the current natural range of the species and the only ones recovered east of the Appalachian Mountains. Apparently this is the youngest evidence of *Iva* cultivation. Its cultivation may have continued here after it was dropped farther west, perhaps indicating either that the habitat here was less suitable for corn or that the Appalachian Summit was something of a backwater area relative to some of the Mississippian developments to the south and west. The history of cultivated sumpweed appears to be similar to that of cultivated sunflower, though the latter persisted to the present.

Cane is not well represented in the samples, and the fragments are all small. Apparently this is *Arundinaria (A. gigantea* or *A. tecta)*.

The vast majority of the unidentified material is composed of two kinds of easily recognized carbonized substances. The largest amount, approximately 10 grams, is from Feature 56. It has the appearance of thin, wrinkled, knobby bark but probably is not. The bulk of the unidentified material from Feature 7, approximately 3 grams, has somewhat the appearance of thick, fleshy leaf. It is composed of a multitude of long cylindrical cells between thin epidermal layers. This material occurs also in the other features, especially in Features 57 and 140. Except for these two substances, the unidentified material is mostly amorphous and unrecognizable, probably largely carbonized bark, and totals approximately 4 grams.

Flint chips and fish scales are poorly represented as compared to flotation materials from other sites which I have examined, and bone is not abundant. More than half the bone from Feature 136 is carbonized, which is unusual. The ubiquitous small snail shells (1- to 2-mm diameter) are present but are not numerous except in Feature 56. Larger snail shells, usually present, are absent from the samples.

It was surprising to find a complete (3 mm long by 1 mm wide) and undamaged carbonized insect (as yet unidentified) in the sample from Feature 56. Its presence could be an indication of warm season deposition and could have ecological significance as well.

Sifting prior to flotation may be responsible for the relatively low representations of stone and animal remains. In fact, the samples were relatively clean and easy to work with, almost all soil having been previously removed. Such cleaning is helpful to the plant remains analyst; but unfortunately, it ordinarily contributes considerably to fragmentation of carbonized material. Screening and flotation are essential but not entirely satisfactory techniques for the recovery of carbonized material.

APPENDIX B

FAUNAL REMAINS FROM THE WARREN WILSON SITE

Elizabeth S. Wing

A sample of faunal remains associated with the Pisgah occupation at the Warren Wilson site provides us with information about the use of animal resources by this late prehistoric Cherokee village. The site is located in Buncombe County, North Carolina, near the Swannanoa River, which offers a source of aquatic vertebrates in addition to land vertebrates. On the basis of these faunal materials there was evidently almost four times as much hunting as fishing. An important element included among these remains is what I consider "incidental animals," too small to have been food.

The faunal remains were excavated from four houses. Within these houses the animal remains are associated with features such as depressions, pits, and burials. In the entire site a total of 208 minimum numbers of individuals of 30 different species are represented (Table B-1).

For analysis of this faunal assemblage the species have been grouped according to their probable economic role. The groups are large game, small game, fur bearers, aquatic species, and incidental species. The first group, large game, consists of only white-tailed deer *(Odocoileus virginianus)*. Small game, the second group, comprises opposum *(Didelphis virginiana)*; rabbit *(Sylvilagus* sp.); woodchuck *(Marmota monax)*; squirrel, both fox and gray *(Sciurus* sp., *Sciurus niger, Sciurus carolinensis)*; turkey *(Meleagris gallopavo)*; and box turtle *(Terrapene carolina)*. The box turtle is the most abundantly represented in this group. The third category is the fur bearers. They are all carnivores and may not necessarily have been used exclusively for fur. Included are gray fox *(Urocyon cinereoargenteus)*, raccoon *(Procyon lotor)*, bear *(Ursus americanus)*, least weasel *(Mustela rixosa)*, bobtail cat *(Lynx rufus)*, and puma *(Felis concolor)*. The aquatic species include beaver *(Castor canadensis)*, frog *(Rana* sp.), hellbender *(Cryptobranchus alleganiensis)*, brown water snake *(Natrix* sp.), mud snake

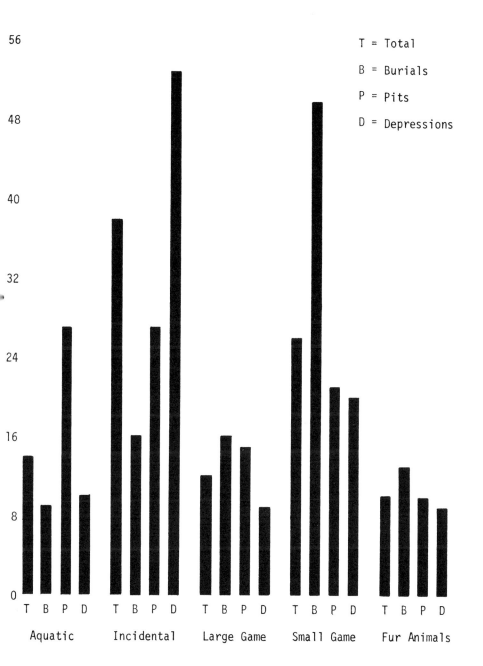

FIGURE B-1. Distribution of animal kinds.

Table B-1. Faunal List

Species	House B MNI	%	House C MNI	%	House D MNI	%	House E MNI	%	Palisade & Plow Zone MNI	%	Total MNI	%
Mammals												
Didelphis virginiana	1	1.1	-	-	-	-	-	-	-	-	1	0.5
Sylvilagus sp.	1	1.1	1	2.4	1	2.4	2	13.3	-	-	5	2.4
Castor canadensis	1	1.1	-	-	-	-	-	-	1	4.5	2	1.0
Marmota monax	1	1.1	1	2.4	-	-	-	-	-	-	2	1.0
Sciurus sp.	2	2.3	-	-	1	2.4	2	13.3	-	-	5	2.4
Sciurus niger	2	2.3	-	-	-	-	-	-	-	-	2	1.0
Sciurus carolinensis	3	3.4	2	4.8	1	2.4	-	-	-	-	6	2.9
Unidentified rodent	-	-	5	11.9	4	9.8	-	-	-	-	9	4.3
Peromyscus sp.	-	-	10	23.8	-	-	-	-	-	-	10	4.8
Urocyon cinereoargenteus	-	-	1	2.4	1	2.4	-	-	1	4.5	3	1.4
Procyon lotor	2	2.3	2	4.8	1	2.4	-	-	1	4.5	6	2.9
Ursus americanus	4	4.5	1	2.4	2	4.9	1	6.7	1	4.5	9	4.3
Mustela rixosa	1	1.1	-	-	-	-	-	-	-	-	1	0.5
Lynx rufus	1	1.1	-	-	-	-	-	-	-	-	1	0.5
Felis concolor	1	1.1	-	-	-	-	-	-	-	-	1	0.5
Odocoileus virginianus	8	9.1	4	9.5	7	17.1	4	26.7	7	31.8	30	14.4
Bird												
Unidentified	4	4.5	3	7.1	2	4.9	-	-	1	4.5	10	4.8

	N	%	N	%	N	%	N	%	N	%	N	%
Unidentified	-	-	-	-	1	2.4	1	6.7	-	-	2	1.0
Bufo sp.	24	27.3	5	11.9	1	2.4	-	-	2	9.1	32	15.4
Rana sp.	2	2.3	-	-	-	-	-	-	1	4.5	3	1.4
Cryptobranchus alleganiensis	1	1.1	-	-	-	-	-	-	-	-	1	0.5
Snake												
Unidentified	1	1.1	-	-	-	-	-	-	-	-	1	0.5
Colubridae	1	1.1	-	-	-	-	-	-	1	4.5	2	1.0
Farancia abacura	-	-	-	-	1	2.4	-	-	-	-	1	0.5
Masticophus flagellum	-	-	1	2.4	-	-	-	-	-	-	1	0.5
Lampropeltis sp.	-	-	1	2.4	1	2.4	-	-	-	-	2	1.0
Natrix sp.	2	2.3	1	2.4	1	2.4	-	-	1	4.5	5	2.4
Heterodon sp.	1	1.1	-	-	-	-	-	-	-	-	1	0.5
Crotalidae	3	3.4	-	-	-	-	1	6.7	-	-	4	1.9
Turtle												
Chrysemys sp.	1	1.1	-	-	-	-	-	-	-	-	1	0.5
Chelydra serpentina	2	2.3	-	-	-	-	-	-	-	-	2	1.0
Terrapene carolina	11	12.5	-	-	4	9.8	2	13.3	3	13.6	20	9.6
Fish												
Catastomidae	2	2.3	1	2.4	10	24.4	-	-	1	4.5	14	6.7
Ictalurus sp.	-	-	1	2.4	-	-	-	-	-	-	1	0.5
Total	88		42		41		15		22		208	

MNI = Minimum number of individuals

(Farancia abacura), snapping turtle *(Chelydra serpentina)*, terrapin *(Chrysemys* sp.), suckers *(Catastomidae)*, and catfish *(Icatalurus* sp.). The last group, the incidental species, I would consider either accidental inclusions in the fauna or granary pests. In this group are small unidentified birds, unidentified mice, deer mouse *(Peromyscus* sp.), toad *(Bufo* sp.), unidentified amphibia and snakes, whip snake *(Masticophis flagellum)*, king snake *(Lampropeltris* sp.), hognose snake *(Heterodon* sp.), and unidentified viper *(Crotalidae)*.

The relative abundance of each of these groups differs in the three archaeological contexts: depressions, pits, and burials (Table B-2). House B, which contains all three kinds of contexts, has a faunal composition virtually identical to that for the entire site. The relative abundances of large game and fur bearers are very similar in these three kinds of contexts, whereas the relative abundances of aquatic, incidental, and small game animals differ considerably. More than twice as many aquatic forms are represented in the pits than in the burials or depressions. Incidental animals are far more abundant in the depressions than elsewhere, and small game species, largely constituting box turtles, are very abundantly represented in the burials.

What these observed characteristics of the fauna mean in terms of man-animal relations can only be tentatively suggested; larger samples are required for verification. This sample clearly indicates an emphasis on hunting as a supplement to agriculture. The unusually large number of carnivores represented in the site does, as indicated, suggest use perhaps primarily for their fur.

Small game animals are particularly associated with the three burials. Box turtle is the most abundant small game animal, but is no more abundantly represented in the burials than in other parts of the site. There is no obvious reason for this apparent association of small game animals with burials.

An association exists between incidental animals and the depressions revealed by excavation. One of these (Feature 7) was evidently a garbage-filled pit along the palisade, while the other (Feature 57) was a depression in the floor of a small structure. Both probably acted as pit traps for the small animals included in the group designated incidental.

To reiterate, the interpretations I have made are preliminary, based upon small samples. What they suggest above all is that a study of larger faunal samples from this site promises to reveal a variety of man-animal relationships, such as hunting for meat and fur; fishing; gathering animals such as turtles, frogs, and snakes by hand; and attracting household fauna (those animals that were attracted to the houses or discarded food debris).

Table B-2. Distribution of Animal Kinds.

Site	Aquatic #	%	Incidental #	%	Large Game #	%	Small Game #	%	Fur #	%	Total #
House B	11	12.5	34	38.6	8	9.1	26	29.5	9	10.2	88
House C	3	7.2	25	59.5	4	9.5	6	14.3	4	9.5	42
House D	12	29.3	9	22.0	7	17.0	9	22.0	4	9.8	41
House E	0	0	2	13.8	4	26.2	8	53.8	1	6.2	15
Total	26	14.0	70	37.6	23	12.4	49	26.3	18	9.7	186
Depressions (7, 57)	9	9.8	49	53.3	8	8.7	18	19.6	8	8.7	92
Burials (3, 7, 15)	3	9.4	5	15.6	5	15.6	15	46.9	4	12.5	32
Pits (53, 136, 137)	14	26.9	14	26.9	8	15.4	11	21.2	5	9.6	52
Postmolds (House E)	0	0	2	13.8	4	26.2	8	53.8	1	6.2	15
Total (186 MNI)	26	14.0	70	37.6	23	12.4	49	26.3	18	9.7	186
Palisade	3		4		4		3		0		14
Plow Zone	1		0		3		1		3		8
TOTAL	30	14.4	74	35.6	30	14.4	53	25.5	21	10.1	208

MNI = Minimum number of individuals

References

Adair, James. 1775. *Adair's History of the American Indian.* 1930 reissue ed. Samuel Cole Williams. Watauga, Johnson City, Tenn.

Bartram, William. 1791. *Travels of William Bartram.* 1940 reissue ed. Mark Van Doren. Dover, New York.

Binford, Lewis R. 1962. "Archaeology as Anthropology." *American Antiquity* 28 (2), 217-225.

Bragg, Laura M. 1918. "Indian Mound Excavation in South Carolina." *Bulletin of the Charleston Museum* 14 (4), 17-20.

Braun, E. Lucy. 1964. *Deciduous Forests of Eastern North America.* Hafner, New York.

Caldwell, Joseph R. 1955. "Cherokee Pottery from Northern Georgia." *American Antiquity* 20 (3), 277-280.

_____. 1958. "Trend and Tradition in the Prehistory of the Eastern United States." *Memoirs of the American Anthropological Association,* no. 88. Menasha, Wis.

Caldwell, Joseph R., and Catherine McCann. 1941. *Irene Mound Site, Chatham County, Georgia.* Univ. of Georgia Press, Athens.

Coe, Joffre L. 1952. "The Cultural Sequence of the Carolina Piedmont." In *Archeology of Eastern United States,* ed. James B. Griffin, pp. 301-311. Univ. of Chicago Press, Chicago.

_____. 1961. Cherokee Archaeology. In "Symposium on Cherokee and Iroquois Culture," ed. John Gulick, pp. 53-60. *Bureau of American Ethnology, Bulletin 180.*

_____. 1964. "The Formative Cultures of the Carolina Piedmont." *Transactions of the American Philosophical Society* 54, pt. 5.

_____. 1969. "Shaft-and-Chamber Burials of the Sixteenth-Century Cherokee." *Abstracts of Papers,* 34th Annual Meeting of the Society for American Archaeology, p. 8.

Coe, Joffre L., and Bennie C. Keel. 1965. "Two Cherokee Houses in Western North Carolina." *Abstracts of Papers,* 30th Annual Meeting of the Society for American Archaeology, p. 5.

Coe, Joffre L., and Ernest Lewis. 1952. "Certain Eastern Siouan Pottery Types." In *Prehistoric Pottery of the Eastern United States,* ed. James P. Griffin, Statement 1-52. Ann Arbor, Mich.

De Baillou, Clemens, and A. R. Kelly. 1960. "Excavation of the Presumptive Site of Estatoe." *Southern Indian Studies* 12, pp. 3-30.

Deetz, James. 1967. *Invitation to Archaeology*. Natural History Press, Garden City, N.Y.

Dickens, Roy S., Jr. 1967a. "The Route of Rutherford's Expedition against the North Carolina Cherokees." *Southern Indian Studies* 19, pp. 3-24.

_____. 1967b. "A Note on Cherokee House Construction of 1776." *Southern Indian Studies* 19, p. 35.

_____. 1970. "The Pisgah Culture and Its Place in the Prehistory of the Southern Appalachians." Doctoral diss., Dept. of Anthropology, Univ. of North Carolina, Chapel Hill.

Dorwin, John T. 1971. "The Bowen Site: An Archaeological Study of Culture Process in the Late Prehistory of Central Indiana." *Prehistory Research Series* 4 (4). Indiana Historical Society, Indianapolis.

Dunnell, Robert C., Lee H. Hanson, Jr., and Donald L. Hardesty. 1971. "The Woodside Component of the Slone Site, Pike County, Kentucky." *Bulletin of Southeastern Archaeological Conference*, ed. Bettye J. Broyles, no. 14.

Egloff, Brian John. 1967. "An Analysis of Ceramics from Historic Cherokee Towns." Master's thesis, Dept. of Anthropology, Univ. of North Carolina, Chapel Hill.

Egloff, Keith Touton. 1971. "Methods and Problems of Mound Excavation in the South Appalachian Area." Master's thesis, Dept. of Anthropology, Univ. of North Carolina, Chapel Hill.

Fairbanks, Charles H. 1946. "The Macon Earth Lodge." *American Antiquity* 12 (2), 94-108.

Ferguson, Leland Greer. 1971. "South Appalachian Mississippian." Doctoral diss., Dept. of Anthropology, Univ. of North Carolina, Chapel Hill.

_____. n.d. "Prehistoric Mica Mines in the Southern Appalachians." Research Laboratories of Anthropology, Univ. of North Carolina, Chapel Hill.

Files of the Research Laboratories of Anthropology, Univ. of North Carolina, Chapel Hill.

Files of the Valentine Museum, Richmond, Va.

Garrow, Patrick H. n.d. "The Mouse Creek 'Focus': A Reevaluation." Paper presented at the King Site Symposium, Southeastern Archaeological Conference, Atlanta, October 1974.

Garrow, Patrick H., and Marvin T. Smith. 1973. *The King Site (9F1-5) Excavations, April, 1971, through August, 1973: Collected Papers*. Dennis Hodge's Office Supply Co., Rome, Ga.

Griffin, James B. 1952. *Archeology of Eastern United States*. Univ. of Chicago Press, Chicago.

_____. 1966. "The Fort Ancient Aspect: Its Cultural and Chronological Position in Mississippi Valley Archaeology." *Anthropological Papers of the Museum of Anthropology, The University of Michigan*, no. 28. Ann Arbor.

_____. 1967. "Eastern North American Archaeology: A Summary." *Science* 156 (3772), 175-191.

Harrington, M. R. 1922. "Cherokee and Earlier Remains on the Upper Tennessee River." *Indian Notes and Monographs.* Museum of the American Indian, Heye Foundation, New York.

Heye, George G. 1919. "Certain Mounds in Haywood County, North Carolina." *Contributions from the Museum of the American Indian, Heye Foundation* 5, (3), 35-43.

Heye, George G., F. W. Hodge, and G. H. Pepper. 1918. "The Nacoochee Mound in Georgia." *Contributions from the Museum of the American Indian, Heye Foundation* 2 (1).

Holden, Patricia Padgett. 1966. "An Archaeological Survey of Transylvania County, North Carolina." Master's thesis, Dept. of Anthropology, Univ. of North Carolina, Chapel Hill.

Holland, C. G. 1970. "An Archaeological Survey of Southwest Virginia." *Smithsonian Contributions to Anthropology,* no. 12. Smithsonian Institution Press, Washington, D. C.

Holmes, William H. 1884. "Illustrated Catalogue of a Portion of the Collections Made by the Bureau of Ethnology during the Field Season of 1881." *Third Annual Report of the Bureau of Ethnology, 1881-82,* pp. 427-510. Washington, D. C.

_____. 1903. "Aboriginal Pottery of the Eastern United States." *Twentieth Annual Report of the Bureau of American Ethnology, 1898-99.* Washington, D. C.

Keel, Bennie C. 1967. "Garden Creek Mound, Hw 2, Haywood County, North Carolina." *Abstracts of Papers,* 32nd Annual Meeting of the Society for American Archaeology, p. 4.

_____. 1972. "Woodland Phases of the Appalachian Summit Area." Doctoral diss., Dept. of Anthropology, Washington State Univ., Pullman.

Keel, Bennie C., and Jefferson Chapman. n.d. "The Cultural Position of the Connestee Phase in Southeastern Prehistory." Research Laboratories of Anthropology, Univ. of North Carolina, Chapel Hill.

Keeler, Robert Winston. 1971. "An Archaeological Survey of the Upper Catawba River Valley." Honors' thesis, Dept. of Anthropology, Univ. of North Carolina, Chapel Hill.

Kellar, James H. 1967. "Part 3, Material Remains." In *Angel Site: An Archaeological, Historical, and Ethnological Study, Vol. II,* by Glenn Black, pp. 431-487. Indiana Historical Society, Indianapolis.

Kelly, A. R., and Lewis H. Larson, Jr. 1957. "Explorations at Etowah, Georgia, 1954-1956." *Archaeology* 10 (1), 39-48.

Kelly, A. R., and R. S. Neitzel. 1961. "The Chauga Site in Oconee County, South Carolina." *University of Georgia Laboratory of Archaeology Series,* Report no. 3. Athens.

Kneberg, Madeline. 1952. "The Tennessee Area." In *Archeology of Eastern United States,* ed. James B. Griffin, pp. 190-198. Univ. of Chicago Press, Chicago.

_____. 1959. "Engraved Shell Gorgets and Their Associations." *Tennessee Archaeologist* 15 (1), 1-39.

Kroeber, A. L. 1939. "Cultural and Natural Areas of Native North America." *University of California Publications in American Archaeology and Ethnology* 38.

Larson, Lewis H., Jr. 1971. Archaeological Implications of Social Stratification at the Etowah Site, Georgia. In "Approaches to the Social Dimensions of Mortuary Practices," ed. James A. Brown. *Memoirs of the Society for American Archaeology,* no. 25, pp. 58-67. Washington, D. C.

_____. 1972. "Functional Considerations of Warfare in the Southeast during the Mississippian Period." *American Antiquity* 37 (3), 383-392.

Lewis, T. M. N., and Madeline Kneberg. 1941. "The Prehistory of the Chickamauga Basin in Tennessee." *Tennessee Anthropological Papers,* no. 1 (mimeographed). Division of Anthropology, Univ. of Tennessee, Knoxville.

_____. 1946. *Hiwassee Island: An Archaeological Account of Four Tennessee Indian Peoples.* Univ. of Tennessee Press, Knoxville.

_____. 1957. "The Camp Creek Site." *Tennessee Archaeologist* 13 (1), 1-48.

_____. 1958. *Tribes That Slumber.* Univ. of Tennessee Press, Knoxville.

MacNeish, Richard S. 1952. "Iroquois Pottery Types: A Technique for the Study of Iroquois Pottery." *National Museum of Canada, Bulletin No. 124.*

McCord, Howard A., Jr. 1966. "The McLean Mound, Cumberland County, North Carolina." *Southern Indian Studies* 18, pp. 1-45.

Muller, Jon D. 1966. "Archaeological Analysis of Art Styles." *Tennessee Archaeologist* 22 (1), 25-39.

Myers, Richard. 1961. "Important Discovery at the Cox Site Excavation." *Tennessee Archaeologist* 17 (1), 22-25.

Neumann, Georg K. 1942. "Types of Artificial Cranial Deformation in the Eastern United States." *American Antiquity* 7 (3), 306-310.

Osborne, A. J. n.d. "Osborne's Report [to B. B. Valentine] Regarding Opening of Mound on George Smathers' Land, Haywood County, North Carolina in 1880." Original document on file at the Valentine Museum, Richmond, Va.

Peattie, Roderick. 1943. *The Great Smokies and the Blue Ridge: The Story of the Southern Appalachians.* Vanguard, New York.

Perkinson, Phil H. 1971. "North Carolina Fluted Projectile Points: Survey Report Number One." *Southern Indian Studies* 23, pp. 3-40.

Polhemus, Richard R. n.d. Field Notes on Excavations at Cobb Island and McCullough Bend Sites, Tennessee.

Polhemus, Richard R., and James H. Polhemus. 1966. "The McCullough Bend Site." *Tennessee Archaeologist* 22 (1), 13-24.

Records Relating to the Affairs of the Valentine Brothers, 1879-1880s.

Reid, James Jefferson, Jr. 1967. "Pee Dee Pottery from the Mound at Town Creek." Master's thesis, Dept. of Anthropology, Univ. of North Carolina, Chapel Hill.

Runquist, Jeannette. 1970. "Archaeological Skeletal Material: A Study in the Methods of Excavation, Preservation, Reassembly and Analysis." Master's thesis, Dept. of Anthropology, Univ. of North Carolina, Chapel Hill.

Sanford, Patricia. 1970. "An Ethnobotanical Study of the Fawcett [Warren Wilson] Site." Honors' thesis, Dept. of Anthropology, Univ. of North Carolina, Chapel Hill.

Sears, William H. 1955. "Creek and Cherokee Culture in the 18th Century." *American Antiquity* 21 (2), 143-149.

_____. 1958. "The Wilbanks Site (9Ck-5), Georgia." *Bureau of American Ethnology, Bulletin 169,* pp. 129-194.

_____. 1968. "The State and Settlement Patterns in the New World." In *Settlement Archaeology,* ed. K. C. Chang, pp. 134-153. National Press Books, Palo Alto, Calif.

Sears, William H., and James B. Griffin. 1950. "Fiber-Tempered Pottery of the Southeast." In *Prehistoric Pottery of Eastern United States,* ed. James B. Griffin, Statement 6-50. Ann Arbor, Mich.

Service, Elman R. 1962. *Primitive Social Organization: An Evolutionary Perspective.* Random House, New York.

Setzler, Frank M., and Jesse D. Jennings. 1941. "Peachtree Mound and Village Site, Cherokee County, North Carolina." *Bureau of American Ethnology, Bulletin 131.*

Shelford, Victor E. 1963. *The Ecology of North America.* Univ. of Illinois Press, Urbana.

Smith, David C., and Frank M. Hodges, Jr. 1968. "The Rankin Site, Cocke County, Tennessee." *Tennessee Archaeologist* 24 (2), 37-91.

Smithsonian Institution, Museum of Natural History, Photographic Laboratory, Negative 37318-E.

Thomas, Cyrus. 1887. "Work in Mound Exploration of the Bureau of Ethnology," *Bureau of Ethnology, Bulletin 4.*

_____. 1890. *The Cherokees in Pre-Columbian Times.* N. D. C. Hodges, Publisher, New York.

_____. 1891. "Catalog of Prehistoric Works East of the Rocky Mountains," *Bureau of American Ethnology, Bulletin 12.*

_____. 1894. "Report on the Mound Explorations of the Bureau of American Ethnology." *Twelfth Annual Report of the Bureau of American Ethnology, 1890-1891,* pp. 3-730. Washington, D.C.

Thornbury, William D. 1965. *Regional Geomorphology of the United States.* Wiley, New York.

Timberlake, Henry. 1765. *The Memoirs of Lieut. Henry Timberlake.* 1948 reissue ed. Samuel Cole Williams. Continental Book Co., Marietta, Ga.

Valentine, Edward P. n.d. "Report [to M. S. Valentine] on Excavations at the Sawnooke Mound, Swain County, North Carolina in 1882." Original document on file at the Valentine Museum, Richmond, Va.

Valentine, G. G., B. B. Valentine, and E. P. Valentine. 1898. "Catalog of Objects." In *The Valentine Museum* [museum handbook]. Richmond, Va.

Wauchope, Robert. 1948. "The Ceramic Sequence in the Etowah Drainage, Northwest Georgia." *American Antiquity* 13 (3), 201-209.

_____. 1966. "Archaeological Survey of Northern Georgia: With a Test of Some Cultural Hypotheses." *Memoirs of the Society for American Archaeology,* no. 21.

Webb, William S. 1938. "An Archaeological Survey of the Norris Basin in Eastern Tennessee." *Bureau of American Ethnology, Bulletin 118.*

Webb, William S., and David L. DeJarnette. 1942. "An Archaeological Survey of Pickwick Basin in the Adjacent Portions of the States of Alabama, Mississippi and Tennessee." *Bureau of American Ethnology, Bulletin 129.*

Whiteford, Andrew H. 1952. "A Frame of Reference for the Archaeology of Eastern Tennessee." In *Archeology of Eastern United States,* ed. James B. Griffin, pp. 207-225. Univ. of Chicago Press, Chicago.

Willey, Gordon R., and Philip Phillips. 1958. *Method and Theory in American Archaeology.* Univ. of Chicago Press, Chicago.

Wilms, Douglas C. 1974. "Cherokee Settlement Patterns in Nineteenth Century Georgia." *Southeastern Geographer* 14 (1), 46-53.

Wilson, Rex L. 1964. "A Radiocarbon Date for the Macon Earthlodge." *American Antiquity* 30 (2), 202-203.

Yarnell, Richard A. 1972. "*Iva annua* var. *macrocarpa:* Extinct American Cultigen?" *American Anthropologist* 74 (3), 335-341.

Index

THE UNIVERSITY OF TENNESSEE PRESS